A WORLD UNBROKEN

HOPE AND HEALING FOR A SHATTERED WORLD

Chris Folmsbee and Jason Sivewright

bare
foot
MINISTRIES

Copyright 2011 by Barefoot Ministries®, Kansas City, Missouri

ISBN 978-0-8341-5049-2

Printed in the United States of America

Editor: Audra Marvin

Creative Editorial Contributions: Aaron Mitchum, Paul Sheneman, Mike Wonch, Laurey Kiehne

Cover & Interior Design: Mark Novelli, IMAGO

Library of Congress Control Number: 2010937896

10 9 8 7 6 5 4 3 2 1

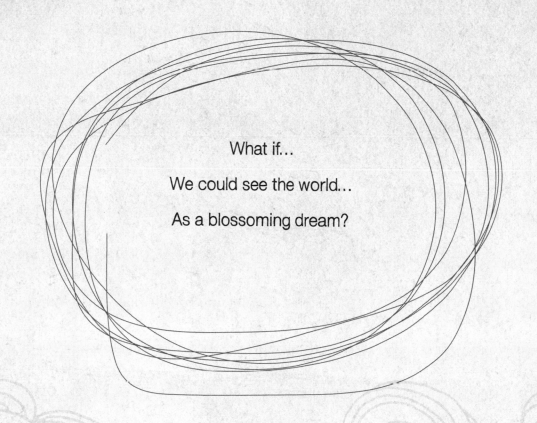

What if...

We could see the world...

As a blossoming dream?

I Stumbled upon a crumpled up Something.

I could call it a blossoMinG DReam

I picked it up and put it in my pocket.

And Now it is always with me.

4

So now we begin.

I can imagine that people will flip through this book and call us crazy. How can we possibly think that you might be interested in all of this? The time commitment, the courage, and the motivation it will take to complete this experience will be immense. This will be hard. This will be a struggle. But it might just be the struggle that defines your life.

What might happen to your church? What might happen to your campus, your community, the world, if you embrace this mission and encourage others to do the same?

Look around you. This world is just as full of pictures of God as it is pictures of his broken intentions for us, his creation. And whether you realize it or not, you have been included in a story that began long ago and is still being written today. It is a story of things lost and things found. It is a story of great sorrow and great hope. But above all, it is a story of love, and it requires your response.

It is not enough for you to be moderately or relevantly interested in things like holiness, compassion, social justice, and environmental stewardship.

Encountering the story of God and embracing God's mission means being swept up in a wave with no certain path but a certain destination.

So look around you.

What if…
We could see the world…
As a blossoming dream?

HOW TO MOVE THROUGH THE *WORLD UNBROKEN* EXPERIENCE:

Rules: Well...there is really just one. Pray like crazy and use this book as your own personal journal, sketchbook, coloring book, notepad, or whatever. Some of the actions will take more than a day, and others won't. Some you may not be able to do. Some won't interest you at all, and others will spark your imagination. Be faithful with your effort in all these things, and you will see God moving through you and your creative community.

pray The pray section is set up for you as a guide to your daily prayer life. Feel free to add your own words or write a completely new prayer in response to what God is doing in your life through this experience.

act These are the things you do. Some of it will seem crazy, but how long has it been since you have embraced the opportunity to be courageous? If your prayers are bold, then your actions must follow. Go and make it so.

sketch Okay, so we designated an area for you to respond however you see fit, but in truth, this whole book is a sketch area. Feel free to use it as such.

Read these prayers and remember this page. You will become very familiar with them throughout this experience. Maybe you'll want to flip back to this page each week. For those slightly more daring...memorize them or rewrite them as you move along.

EVERY 6TH DAY PRAYER

Father,
Make me an agent of restoration.
Allow me to believe in a world unbroken
Rather than lining up with the masses to mourn a broken world.
I commit myself to this year of prayers and action
because I believe in something bigger.
I believe that change can take place,
And not just a change in me because this isn't about me,
But a change in the world around me.
I commit myself to seeking you everywhere.
In every face and every flower, every laugh and every cry.
I commit myself to listening.
And when I have learned to listen,
I pray that you will teach me how to lead.
"Your kingdom come, your will be done.
On earth as it is in heaven."

Amen

EVERY 7TH DAY PRAYER

Creator God,
I rest in you today.
You are big.
You are great.
And I praise you
Forever and ever.

Amen

God spoke:
"Lights! Come out!

Shine in Heaven's sky!

Separate Day from Night.

Mark seasons and days and years,

Lights in Heaven's sky

to give light to Earth."

And there it was.

—GENESIS 1:14-15 (THE MESSAGE)

create

pray

THIS MORNING I PRAY...

Reside over the dark places in my life today, God.
And to these places, bring light.
A light that reminds me of my original purpose
    and my original design:
To be more like you, my Creator.
Help me today to be aware of the
    dazzling pictures of your creative spirit...
Everywhere.
Amen

THIS DAY I PRAY...

Today, Father
Begin something new in my life.
Amen

THIS NIGHT I PRAY...

My Creator God,
I thank you for making me in your image.
I pray tonight that as I begin this journey
I might take your lead and bring light to
    all the dark places around me.
In my speaking of words. In my relationships.
In my sports teams. In my singing of songs.
In my family. In my community.
In my church. In my everyday, ordinary life...
I pray that I will always strive to participate
    in the creation and restoration of your vast
    and wondrous masterpiece—
    your world and your people.
Thank you for all of this.
Amen

act

BEGINNINGS...
HERE ARE THREE OPTIONS (PLEASE CHOOSE ONE, TWO, OR ALL THREE).

 **Plant something**—any kind of plant, whether it be just for beauty (e.g., roses) or something that bears fruit (e.g., strawberry plant). As you do so, think about how God made us, not only as created beings but created beings who then partner in the creation process.

Begin a friendship—with someone you don't know or an occasional acquaintance. Maybe even someone you wouldn't usually talk to. Make a commitment to nurture this relationship no matter what. (Warning: this is not an excuse to hit on someone of the opposite sex.)

Paint—or don't. Buy or make a large canvas or something like it and hang it on the wall of your bedroom. Add one thing to it every day. This can be anything: one stroke of a paint brush, a smear of dirt, a written word, a chewed piece of gum, etc. At the top write these words: *A Portrait of His Creation...(your name, nickname, or initials)*.

sketch

Stop at some point today and look around you. Document below what you see, hear, feel, sense; people, trees, the wind, animals, the smells, the sky, cars, creation moving around you. These are the fingerprints of God—proof of his amazingly creative personality. Try and grasp that.

pray

THIS MORNING I PRAY...

Creator God,

Thank you for shining your light in love, Father.

I pray that in my bringing of light,
  you will fill me with that same love.

That love that hovered over the darkness
  and cared enough to create life.

Give me sight, Father

The kind of sight that seeks out the wounded and the broken

The kind of sight that seeks out the dead places
  and longs to bring healing and restoration

The kind of sight that seeks out darkness
  but never accepts it

The kind of sight that reaches out like you did.

Amen

THIS DAY I PRAY...

Creator,

"Oh my God, shine your light on us, that we might live"

"Oh my God, shine your light on us, that we might live"

"Oh my God, shine your light on us, that we might live"

Amen

THIS NIGHT I PRAY...

Creator God,

I pray that you would shine on me at full strength.

That you might know every place in my being.

Open my eyes, Father, to the dead places around me that
  I have been blind to all my life.

The lack of justice. The lack of mercy. The lack of light.

I humbly ask that you would make me a beacon of love
  and life to these vast dark places.

"Oh my God, shine your light on us, that we might live."*

*From "Shine Your Light on Us." Robbie Seay Band. *Give Yourself Away.* Sparrow Records

act

Write a note that you can give to anyone. It doesn't have to be long. In fact, it probably shouldn't be. In it, explain how God loved that person so much that he created the world..

Pray. Pray that God will reveal to you a place of great darkness. (If you are lost on this one, here are some suggestions: a homeless shelter, a meeting for people with substance abuse issues, a hospital ward, a person you know is dealing with a loss... But don't just pick one flippantly. Honestly pray and allow God to direct your actions.)

Go to that place and choose a person. Give that person the note and walk away.

sketch

Use this space to define the characteristics of light with shapes, pictures, colors, or words. What is it about light that changes things? Document some places in your life that are vastly different when the light is present.

God set them in the expanse of the sky to give light on the earth, to govern the day and the night, and to separate light from darkness. And God saw that it was good.

—GENESIS 1:17-18 (NIV)

pray

THIS MORNING I PRAY…

Father,
I stand amazed in the vastness of you.
I look to the sky and I am overwhelmed by your beauty.
I look to the sea and I am surrounded by your power.
I can't believe a God who is so big
    has taken the time to love me.
Thank you for all of this.
Amen

THIS DAY I PRAY…

Father,
Thank you for taking pleasure in amazing me
    with your creation.
Amen

THIS NIGHT I PRAY…

Creator God,
As I stand in awe of all you have done,
    I ask humbly for your help.
I pray that you will help me to understand
    my place in creation.
Help me be a better steward of this world
    you have given me to take care of.
Like the cultivator of a great masterpiece,
    make my hands both gentle and swift,
    both powerful and loving.
Help me to understand, as I look to the stars,
    that this is not about me.
Yet I am a part…
Part of a vast and wonderful story unfolding
    all around me.
Thank you for all of this.
Amen

act

Get together with a friend or a group of friends today and discuss what amazes you about the bigness of God.

sketch

Watch the clouds. In this space, draw your favorite ones. Thinking about the clouds, the stars, thunderstorms, sunsets—list some reasons that God might have had for making the sky look the way it does.

pray

THIS MORNING I PRAY...

O, Creator,
Today I breathe deeply.
I commit myself to examining life.
The plant in my living room or the tree in my backyard.
My pet goldfish, my awesome dog,
    the raccoon that tips over my trashcans,
    or the lions on the Discovery™ channel.
I wonder at the cycle of it all, Father.
How it is constantly moving.
I praise you for it all.
Amen

THIS DAY I PRAY...

Creator God,
Thank you for making all of this just to amaze me.
To make me laugh. To make me cry.
To make me feel comfort. To help me understand loss.
To help me to see little pictures of your enormous love
    that is always with me.
I am amazed.
Amen

THIS NIGHT I PRAY...

You created the world like a poem.
With the animals and the trees,
The sky and the stars, The storms and the sunsets.
And you weaved your image in and around every word
And you implanted it,
Your image
In me.
Help me understand what that means.

Amen

act

DO ONE OR BOTH OF THESE THINGS:

Hang out with your pet or pets, or offer to watch a friend's pet for an extended amount of time (maybe an hour or more). And really watch the animals. Then imagine they can talk. Think of some questions you might want to ask them about their existence and why they believe they were created. In your sketch space write some of the answers you think they might have.

Climb a tree. Imagine that the tree can talk. Think of some questions you might want to ask the tree about its existence and why it believes it might have been created. In the space below, jot down some of the answers you think it might have.

sketch

pray

THIS MORNING I PRAY…

My Father,
Today I commit myself to standing in awe of you
By standing in awe of the created me.
My prayer for today and every day
Is that people will look at me and see you.
That they will see the things I do and praise my Creator
The one whose image I bear.
Amen

THIS DAY I PRAY…

Creator God,
Help me to see your face in the face of my neighbors
     (every person).
Amen

THIS NIGHT I PRAY…

O, God,
I ask for your blessing upon these hands.
I pray that you will keep them busy with your work,
However hard it may be or impossible it may seem
Make these hands instruments of
     your wondrous creativity
Your grace and your mercy
I ask for your blessing upon this mind
I pray that you will fill it with thoughts that are good
However they may try to deceive me.
Make this mind a vessel of purity and truth
Prepared to go where you and only you might lead
I ask for your blessing upon this heart
That you will fill it with compassion for
     those in the darkness
Continue your work through me.
Amen

act

Investigate: Start by asking yourself these questions. Where do you see God in your… Body? Mind and imagination? Heart and soul?

Ask the same questions of three other people (one friend, one stranger, one adult mentor). Use the space below to write down their thoughts.

Plant a vegetable garden in your neighborhood and invite your friends and neighbors to add whatever they would like to plant. This will not only make your community more environmentally healthy but will also help you create new relationships with your brothers and sisters.

sketch

body

mind & imagination

heart & soul

13

pray

THIS MORNING I PRAY…
Creator God,
I pray today and every day,
Continue your work in me.
Amen

THIS DAY I PRAY…
Father God,
Thank you for seeing in me something
    that I might never have seen in myself…
An artist.
A creator of beautiful things.
Thank you for joining us
    together in this ambition.
The ambition to continue to create,
    design, and color this world.
I pray that all of my creations you might see
And say that it is good.
Amen

THIS NIGHT I PRAY…
Prayer on page 6

act

Whether by yourself or with a group of friends, create something from nothing today. It may be as simple as a paper airplane or as complex as a song, a dance, or a story. It may be a video with friends or a doghouse out of some old, reclaimed plywood.

Whatever it may be, create it and then document how you feel after in the sketch space. Ask yourself these questions:

Why do you think we are able to create things out of nothing?

Why do you think it is sometimes hard for us to do?

Why do you think we find satisfaction in creating?

What other creations inspired your creation? How does this link us all together?

If you are with a group, ask them the same questions and document their responses.

 Use old pillowcases to make tote bags to take to the grocery store, the gym, and school—anywhere you need to carry stuff. Be creative in your decorations so that people are inspired to do the same.

sketch

PLEASE GO TO PAGE 6 FOR MORNING PRAYER

By the seventh day God had finished the work he had been doing; so on the seventh day he rested from all his work. And God blessed the seventh day and made it holy, because on it he rested from all the work of creating that he had done.

—GENESIS 2:2-3 (NIV)

So God created man in his own image,
in the image of God he created him;
male and female he created them.

—GENESIS 1:27 (NIV)

pray

THIS MORNING I PRAY...

Creator God,
Help me to understand that with every choice
    I make, I am establishing a rhythm.
And this rhythm is the rhythm of my life.
I give it you this morning.
I pray that with every breath of my existence
Every passion of my heart
And every creative idea I have
I will be coming closer to falling in step with you.
Begin a new rhythm in me today, Father.
Create in me something new.
Amen

THIS DAY I PRAY...

O God,
Help me to listen to you.
Help me to obey you.
Help me to learn to play along.
Amen

THIS NIGHT I PRAY...

Creator God,
I love you.
And I lift my voice to worship you.
My soul rejoices.
Take joy in what you hear.
My deepest desire is nothing more
Than for my life to be a sweet, sweet sound in your ear.
Amen

act

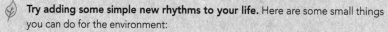

Read through the story of creation in Genesis 1:1-31. See if you can establish a pattern for how God carries out each day in the story—maybe pulling out words, phrases, or actions that take place every day. Write or draw in your sketch space in response.

> Ask yourself...
>
> Why is there a rhythm to the story of creation?
>
> What might this tell us about the way we form our story?

Try adding some simple new rhythms to your life. Here are some small things you can do for the environment:

- Turn the water off while you brush your teeth instead of letting it run.

- Take shorter showers or maybe even shower every other day instead of every day.

- Make sure you turn the light off every time you leave a room.

sketch

pray

THIS MORNING I PRAY…

Mighty Counselor,
Help me in my act of separating,
That my life would no longer be a mass of confusion
But instead you would guide me in bringing form
    to the chaos.
I cannot be everything to everyone.
Please kill my desire to do so.
I pray again
Help me in my act of separating.
Amen

THIS DAY I PRAY…

Counselor,
Give me strength to make the hard decisions
The ones that others don't understand.
Give me clarity.
Give me a kind of peace that only you can give.
Amen

THIS NIGHT I PRAY…

Creator God,
Search my life.
Remove me from the things that remove me from
    you.
Heart, mind, and soul,
So that I might gather my passions into pools of
    light to be used by you.
Just as you gathered the water to reveal dry ground.
Help my life.
In its weird, beautiful, crazy complexity
To begin to take form within your presence.
Amen

act

Hover Above the Abyss. Look at your life. What things cause your story to feel the most chaotic? Take this day to evaluate these things—relationships, desires, habits, hobbies, clubs, groups.

Ask yourself this. *What can I do to separate myself from some of the unneeded chaos in my life?* The symphony of creation begins with God separating. And this is one of the first steps in bringing form to the formlessness. Prayerfully begin that process in your life today. Use the sketch space below to write your thoughts.

 Talk with your parents about having a designated "lights off" time at your house. This will be a time when all use of electric light will end for the day. A cool suggestion: get lots of candles.

sketch

THIS MORNING I PRAY...
Father God,
I long for your direction today.
Help me trust in you with everything I do and say.
As you are with me in my separating.
Be with me in my gathering of revelation.
Show me something new today.
I trust you.
Amen

THIS DAY I PRAY...
Father,
Give me the courage to do what you ask.
Whatever you might ask, give me courage.
I need your help. I can't do it without you.
Amen

THIS NIGHT I PRAY...
Father God,
Create a new rhythm in my life. I am so far from perfect.
I find myself falling into bad relationships, bad habits, bad
    ambitions and desires, over and over.
Establish in me a rhythm of separating and gathering.
Nudge me when I need separation from the things that
    keep me from you.
And in the separation, help me to gather my passions
    again at your feet.
The world may call me crazy.
Help me not to care.
I believe you can do awesome things through me.
Help me with my unbelief.
Help me to bring beautiful form to the densest darkness.
Amen

Today's action is simple. Pray. As you walk through your day, be in constant prayer as you examine your life. In your separating you will be making space. Pray that God will show you new ways he can use your passion for sports, music, writing, Pogo stick jumping, anything. Ask honestly for God to reveal something new to you today. It may be something small. It may be scary big. Gather these revelations and share them with someone you can trust.

The night before trash day, circle your neighborhood and observe how many people are recycling. Those who are not, ask if you can separate their garbage for them. MAKE SURE YOU ASK. And be ready for them to say no, but it might help them think about doing it themselves next time.

19

pray

THIS MORNING I PRAY…

Creator God,

Thank you for creating me with substance.

I praise you for the simple fact that we are not
   shallow creatures.

Though it is sometimes hard to see (fill in the person
   and situation)…

We are all vast and bottomless beings…

Amazing masterpieces…

Full of emotions and stories…

Constantly expanding substance.

I commit myself to the substance of life today.

Amen

THIS DAY I PRAY…

Creator God,

In my forming

Make me brave.

Be with me.

Amen

THIS NIGHT I PRAY…

Holy Spirit,

Fill me to the brim

So that people see me

My community

My actions

My words

And praise you.

Amen

act

Form a Creative Community. This may take longer than a day or a week, but start this action today. On your campus today, begin a very inclusive (everyone's invited) creative community. Make flyers, make announcements, post bulletins. Make it known that you are forming a group that will meet regularly for one purpose and one purpose only: *bringing substance to life.*

This may seem crazy, but as you form this group, drench your actions in prayer, asking God to show you how to proceed. Then just trust. Be creative with the name of your group and the time and place you will meet.

You may do this with friends, but don't allow this to become a clique. Establish the form and take a leap. This could be awesome!

 **Gather together with some friends and take a walk among nature.** As you do, gather things you could use as musical instruments. When you're done, have a symphony of noise with the things you gathered.

sketch

pray

THIS MORNING I PRAY...
Father,
Paint my life with the colors of my community.
Fill my existence with the stories of my neighbor.
I was not made to simply pass it all by.
I was made to breathe it all in
And to exhale encouragement and gentleness.
Help this group, Father
As we form and fill together.
Amen

THIS DAY I PRAY...
Creator God,
Fill my life with the things you would have me do.
Fill the spaces in my life with
    your passions and desires.
Show me what you would have me do.
Amen

THIS NIGHT I PRAY...
Creator God,
Help me to be led by you
In my separating
In my gathering
In my forming
In my filling
And let this be the rhythm of my life.
Amen

act

Meet with your creative community (even if it is just you and a friend) and discuss your purpose: *bringing substance to life.* What does that mean in your context?

Here are some questions to consider:

What can you do as a group to creatively contribute to your community?

What can you do as a group to creatively contribute to an environmental cause in your community or the world?

What can you do as a group to help each other in cultivating good relationships, ambitions, and habits?

Where, when, and how often can you meet?

sketch

"God saw that it was good."

—GENESIS 1:16 (THE MESSAGE)

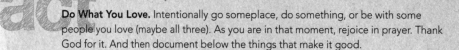

pray

THIS MORNING I PRAY…

Father God,
I pray that I would add to my rhythm
The ability to rejoice in what is good
And to name it as such.
Amen

THIS DAY I PRAY…

Creator God,
I rejoice today in your handiwork
This place
And these people.
Within all of it I see staggering images of you
And I rejoice.
I love you, Lord.
And I lift my voice to worship you.
My soul rejoices.
Take joy in what you hear.
My deepest desire is nothing more
Than for my life to be a sweet sound in your ear.
Amen

THIS NIGHT I PRAY…

Prayer from page 6

act

Do What You Love. Intentionally go someplace, do something, or be with some people you love (maybe all three). As you are in that moment, rejoice in prayer. Thank God for it. And then document below the things that make it good.

 Embrace your inner tree-hugger by actually hugging a tree.

PLEASE GO TO PAGE 6 FOR MORNING PRAYER

By the seventh day God had finished the
work he had been doing; so on the seventh
day he rested from all his work. And God
blessed the seventh day and made it holy,
because on it he rested from all the work of
creating that he had done.

—GENESIS 2:2-3 (NIV)

God took the Man and set him down in the Garden of Eden to work the ground and keep it in order.

—GENESIS 2:15 (THE MESSAGE)

pray

THIS MORNING I PRAY...

Creator God,
Awaken in me a caretaker's heart,
That I might not only be able to name what is good
But begin to feel a greater desire to protect it
With all that I am.
The truth is this—the world is full of you, God.
And if I notice this
I can't be the same anymore.
I am ready to change.
I am ready to return to the garden.
Amen

THIS DAY I PRAY...

Father,
Help me to take pride in your creation
So much so that I hurt when it hurts
So much so that I simply cannot stand aside
And let things remain out of order.
Amen

THIS NIGHT I PRAY...

O God,
When I think about the fact that you made this
    all for my keeping
I feel humbled, overwhelmed, a little scared
A little excited.
I simply don't know where to start.
Show me, Father.
Show me how to be a good steward of
    the awesome gift you gave me.
Amen

act

Think on this. According to the story of creation, God allows Adam to name all the creatures he made, thereby sharing his dominion over earth with us. Have you ever considered that God made you to partner with him in the ownership of this world? You were meant to take pride in the way you take care of God's creation.

Pray about this. Walk around with this idea in your mind today. Ask questions of God if you have them.

Gather with some friends and discuss the idea of Adam naming the animals. Talk about your favorite animals and what you might have named them if it had been you.

In your sketch space, jot down some thoughts that surface as you dwell on these things.

sketch

pray

THIS MORNING I PRAY…
Creator God,
Begin in me a good work
And let it begin today.
Amen

THIS DAY I PRAY…
Father God,
I pray for those who are…
Hurting
Broken
Wounded.
Help me to spend my life seeking them out.
Simply, Lord…
Help me to care more for them than for myself.
Help me to forget myself remembering them.
Amen

THIS NIGHT I PRAY…
Father God,
This is the honest prayer of a caretaker.
That I might never care for others
     because it's hip.
That I might never care for others
     because it benefits me.
That I might care for others
     because I am a steward of creation
And your created ones.
I pray for those (the broken, the lost, the wounded).
May relational stewardship
     become another rhythm of my life.
Amen

act

Relational Stewardship. Chances are, you see something every day that is out of whack—someone getting pushed into a locker; someone sitting alone at lunch; the friend in your group who always seems to get picked on; the person who never has enough money to buy lunch. These are wounds of brokenness.

The sad thing is that you grow so accustomed to seeing these things that you usually pass on by. Accepting the role of a caretaker means giving up the right to pass on by.

I know, this is hard. Take one step toward righting one of these relational wounds today. Ask God to show you the situation, and then, when it arises and you would usually walk on, stop and engage.

 Take steps to make your backyard, front yard, or area around your complex a welcoming habitat for creatures. You can do this by planting trees, bushes, and flowers that are native to your area. Doing this will not only give them a place to feel at home but will also provide them with food.

sketch

pray

THIS MORNING I PRAY…

Creator God,
Continue in me a good work
And let it continue today
And every day.
Amen

THIS DAY I PRAY…

O God,
Forgive me for treating the earth like my own personal
    doormat.
Open my eyes to the wounds that surround me.
Give me the courage to make change real and attainable.
With your help, I believe it can be.
Help me to do it all with love, gentleness, and firm confidence.
Amen

THIS NIGHT I PRAY…

Creator God,
This is the honest prayer of a caretaker.
That I might never care for the earth
    because it's cool.
That I might never care for the earth
    because it benefits me.
That I might care for the earth
    because this is one reason why you put me here.
To work the ground
To be a steward of your creation.
Help me to bring healing by
    whatever means I am capable.
May environmental stewardship become another
    rhythm of my life.
Amen

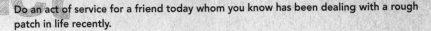

act

Do an act of service for a friend today whom you know has been dealing with a rough patch in life recently.

Chances are, you see something every day. A wound of creation. Sometimes you may even contribute to it. The multiple Styrofoam cups that get used in your cafeteria each day; the hundreds of papers and other recyclable materials that don't get thrown in the recycle bin; the litter in your parking lot; the factory down the street; the bags you use at the supermarket and the non-reusable products that you put in those bags.

The crazy thing is that we learn to just accept these things as unavoidable or imperative to maintaining our comfort level, so we just pass on by. Being a steward of creation means losing some comfort and, again, giving up the right to pass on by.

Take one step today toward righting one of the environmental wounds you observe around you. Pray about what God would have you do, and then be bold in going forward with it.

This might mean making some people mad. It might mean disrupting the natural flow of things by holding some picket signs. Saving the earth is worth some ruffled feathers, as long as it is done in love.

sketch

pray

THIS MORNING I PRAY…

Creator God,
I reflect on the story of creation today.
What great detail you put into everything here.
I can't believe how awesome and intentional everything is.
Everything working together, everything with a purpose.
I thank you for it all.
Might I never take it for granted.
Help me today to begin the process of moving
Away from being a selfish consumer
Toward being a righteous ruler.
Amen

THIS DAY I PRAY…

Counselor,
Awaken in me the spirit of a righteous caretaker.
Amen

THIS NIGHT I PRAY…

Father God,
Help me to always remember
And always embrace this idea:
That my care for creation and created ones
Directly affects my relationship with you.
The measure by which I love this world and these people
Is the measure of my love for you.
I long to love you well, Father.
I long to right the wrongs and heal the wounds
    within my reach.
Help me to do so. I can't do it without you.
Amen

act

On your own or with a group of friends, define the characteristics of two characters as if you were writing a story about each: righteous ruler and selfish consumer. Discuss what each means to you. (Remember: God made a decision to share his dominion over this world with us.)

Now the hard part. On your own, think about how these characters apply to your life. Which do you most relate to? What can you do to relate more to the story of the righteous ruler than to the selfish consumer?

Make a habit of always taking reusable bags to the store instead of using plastic. Offer to go to the store with family and friends and try and influence them to do the same.

sketch

create 19

pray

THIS MORNING I PRAY...
O God,
Help me to see
Amen

THIS DAY I PRAY...
Father God,
I pray again
Today and every day
Help me to see.
Amen

THIS NIGHT I PRAY...
Raise up around me a community of caretakers.
Open our eyes to the environmental and social
    injustices we witness each day.
Help us, as a group, to love you more.
Help us to see.
Help us to see.
O God, help us to see.
Amen

act

VISION. Go somewhere with a friend. Here are some suggestions: a cafe, a restaurant, a park, a street corner. Sit next to one another and look around your environment, using your sketch space write or draw all that you observe.

Do this for five minutes without discussing or showing each other. At the end of the five minutes, share with each other what you observed.

Ask these questions:

How are your observations different?

How are they the same?

What do you think this tells you about vision, the way we see things?

Use the rest of the space to document some thoughts you have. Chances are, especially in a crowded place, your observations were decidedly different. Today, think and pray about these two ideas:

- Being a caretaker of creation has a lot to do with vision, how we see things.

- Being a caretaker was never meant to be done alone. It was meant to be done in community.

sketch

pray

THIS MORNING I PRAY...

Counselor,

Fill me to the brim with love for your creation.

Form in me the true heart of a caretaker.

In my thoughts

In my relationships

In my environment

In my community.

Remove from me the empty visions of the
consumer culture.

Transform them into the blossoming dreams
of the righteous steward.

Make my life a good work.

Amen

THIS DAY I PRAY...

Father God,

Help me never to be the kind who is full of talk.

Instead, help me to act on what I know is right.

Be in the formation of my plans to act

And in the fulfilling of their purpose.

Amen

THIS NIGHT I PRAY...

Prayer from page 6

act

Devise a Plan. Meet with your creative community and discuss environmental and/or relational wounds that you all have observed.

Ask these questions in your group:

How can we creatively work to heal these wounds?

What is our goal in doing so?

How, when, and where can we accomplish this goal, or take steps to accomplish it?

When do we begin?

sketch

PLEASE GO TO PAGE 6 FOR MORNING PRAYER

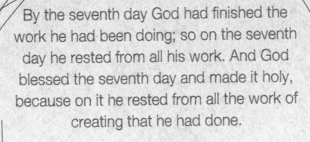

By the seventh day God had finished the work he had been doing; so on the seventh day he rested from all his work. And God blessed the seventh day and made it holy, because on it he rested from all the work of creating that he had done.

—GENESIS 2:2-3 (NIV)

Then the man and his wife heard the sound of the LORD God as he was walking in the garden in the cool of the day.

—GENESIS 3:8 (NIV)

THIS MORNING I PRAY...
Father God,
Help me to remember what it was like
When we walked together in the garden
"in the cool of the day."
In my remembering, help me to long for it again.
Amen

THIS DAY I PRAY...
Father God,
Establish in me a vision of perfection
For this world.
For my life.
For my relationships.
It is a lofty dream.
To be honest, the word scares me.
I don't know that I can understand it...
And I really don't know if I can grasp it completely.
But my purpose holds
To long for nothing less than to return this world to
        the garden—perfect again,
"in the cool of the day."
I believe, with you, it can be done.
Help me with my unbelief.
Amen

THIS NIGHT I PRAY...
Father God,
Help me to be perfect as you are perfect.
Amen

Perfection Defined. In the sketch space below, write down all the thoughts and questions that come to mind when you think of the word *perfect*. Then recall and write down a story from your own life that you would define as perfection. Maybe it was a perfect vacation, a perfect day, or even a perfect moment.

Think and pray on this: *How does the word* perfect *play into your picture of the world and your personal spiritual walk?*

Create a piece of artwork out of recycled materials today. You may want to do this with a group of friends. When you are finished, ask school administrators if you can place the artwork somewhere in your school or on your campus so your fellow students can be reminded of the importance of recycling.

pray

THIS MORNING I PRAY…

As I dwell among creation,
I commit this week to dreaming outside the box.
I commit this day to thinking about what could be.
I am sick of accepting the lie that we are stuck here
In a broken world…so lost…so separated.
Father, help me to imagine a better story.
And help me to share that story with the world.
Amen

THIS DAY I PRAY…

Father God,
Continue to align my desires with yours.
Awaken in me a prophetic image—
    a picture of how things could be.
Amen

THIS NIGHT I PRAY…

O God,
Examine my heart and my desires.
Remove from me anything that isn't
    authentic and genuine.
This is so important
Because if my purpose is not authentic,
    people will smell me out.
They will see right through me.
Remove from me the selfish desires of my heart
And replace them with your dreams
    of restoration for this world.
I love you, Lord.
My soul rejoices, take joy in what you hear.
My deepest desire is nothing more
Than for my life to be a sweet sound in your ear.*
Amen

*Sing to the Lord. Lillenas.

act

Think and pray on this: Usually the word *perfection*—and especially the desire to be perfect—brings with it negative connotations, because we define it based on our own experiences and views. A big part of remembering the garden is aligning our desire for perfection with God's. Simply put, our dreams of the garden must be the same as God's.

Spend an hour or so today pulling weeds in your neighborhood. Weeds can cause pests that suffocate the potential beauty of plants and trees. Clearing them away will, in time, give you a clearer picture of God's handiwork.

Divide your sketch space into two sections. In one section use images, words, or both to describe how you would visualize the garden of Eden. Then read the actual description of the garden from the book of Genesis. Use the other space to describe with images, words, or both what you read.

sketch

pray

act

THIS MORNING I PRAY…

Father God,
Help me to remember that your garden of Eden
involves community.
I was not made to do this alone.
For better or worse, I thank you for that.
And I pray that I can embrace my community
with a love that is…
Bottomless, without stipulations or guidelines,
Completely wide open, never judging,
Always accepting, perfect…Agape.
Amen

THIS DAY I PRAY…

Father God,
Help me not only to accept community as
an important part of creation
But to embrace it as a clear and resonant chord
in the rhythm of my life.
It's not enough for me to be an isolated spiritual person.
I have to get out of my box and engage souls.
Help me to do that. Help me never to grow weary of
listening to the stories of others.
Help me never to grow numb to the suffering of others
Help me never to grow so full of myself that
I won't accept others' help.
Amen

THIS NIGHT I PRAY…

Holy Counselor,
Move in us, move among us, move through us.
Amen

Organize an event/party/get-together. This could be as big as a concert with all the proceeds going to charity, or as small as a couple of friends getting together to play video games or dye each other's hair. The point is to be with and among people. As you do so, observe.

Afterwards, document as much as you can remember about the interactions between the people at your event/party/get-together in the sketch space below.

Were there some conflicts? Were there some struggles or annoyances?

Was there some laughter? What emotions were involved?

Think and pray on this: Community is an essential part of God's garden. God immediately recognizes that it is not good for Adam to be alone. Yet community comes with a lot of hard things sometimes; things you wouldn't exactly associate with perfection. How does it change your views of perfection to think that God's perfection includes community?

Organize a walk-to-school day. This will be a day when your whole school makes a commitment not to drive their cars to school. You can be creative in any way you like with this idea. Maybe it is a bike-to-school day or a carpool contest, where a prize is given to the person who drove with the most people in the car. The important thing is instilling the idea that less driving = less fuel emissions. (If you are not old enough to drive, organize a carpooling effort with the person who usually drives you.)

sketch

pray

THIS MORNING I PRAY…

Father God,
Draw me close, very close to you.
Help me to lean against your chest
And steadily hear the beat of your heart
A heart beating for your children.
Set my heart to the same beat, Father,
So that we might have union like we did in the garden.
Help me to remember what it was like
To walk with you "in the cool of the day."
Amen

THIS DAY I PRAY…

Creator God,
Help me understand what it means
To be in perfect union with you.
This is my prayer today and every day
That I might know you more.
Amen

THIS NIGHT I PRAY…

Father God,
As I move along, help me never to forget.
Help me always to remember how this all began.
That in the beginning we were strolling
    in a garden with you.
My life gets so crazy/mundane…
Busy/boring…
Eventful/eventless…
That sometimes I find it hard to believe.
My prayer is that you would show me
    pictures of the garden…
In my community and in my relationships.
Amen

act

Take a Walk. After the fall, Adam and Eve were hiding when they heard the sound of God "strolling in the garden in the evening breeze." Take a long walk. And as you do, think on these things:

Imagine the sound of God strolling in the garden.

Imagine what it would be like to share that kind of union with God again; to be able to stroll with him in the garden.

How is this different from your relationship with God now?

Does this affect your idea of perfection?

Use your sketch space to respond.

Find a workout partner. This could be someone to go to the gym with, to run with, or just to take a walk with once a week. The important thing isn't only the exercise but getting to know that person on a deeper level.

sketch

pray

THIS MORNING I PRAY…

Father God,
Give me wisdom to choose well.
My life is full of choices.
Messages are coming at me constantly
And I am choosing to accept or ignore.
Give me strength to never let down my guard.
I pray today and every day
That you would help me to know what is good.
Be near in my choosing.
Amen

THIS DAY I PRAY…

Creator God,
I have lots of choices.
Give me the courage to always choose to obey.
And when I fail or choose poorly
Help me never to decide to hide from you
My maker.
Amen

THIS NIGHT I PRAY…

Father God,
I understand that this began with a gift
And a choice.
And it's a choice that I still make every day
To stay with you or to go my own way.
And I ask for your forgiveness tonight
As I find myself outside the garden
Examining life
And dreaming
Longing for Eden again.
Amen

act

Free Will. As you go through your routine today, try and document all the choices you make. Chances are, you will lose track before breakfast, but give it a shot. At the end of the day, look at your long list of choices. Think about what determines the things you choose—saying no or saying yes; accepting or declining; this person or that person; this or that all day long. Why do you think that God gave us the ability to choose? How does this ability play into your picture of the garden of Eden/perfection?

Don't throw anything away today. This will be hard. You might not be able to do it, but trying will open your eyes to the choices you are making every minute that could begin to make you a better steward in the way you consume.

sketch

pray

THIS MORNING I PRAY...

Father God,
As I stand outside the garden,
I pray that I will always remember
To establish a dream of how things were and could be.
To long for God's perfection in my life and relationships.
To embrace community with all its joys and struggles.
And to choose wisely in the face of temptation
    to do otherwise.
Help me, Father
To hope and obey.
To bring healing to the broken.
Amen

THIS DAY I PRAY...

Creator God,
In our brokenness…
Be near.
Amen

THIS NIGHT I PRAY...

Prayer from page 6

act

Shattered Image. With your phone, personal camera, or a disposable camera, take pictures today that remind you of the broken state of the world outside the garden. Keep these pictures in some sort of album (on your phone, computer, or physical photo album) and label the album *Broken*. In your sketch space write the title of each picture and the feelings the image evokes in you.

 Plant Trees. Gather with your creative community and brainstorm a fundraising event that will raise money to buy supplies to plant trees in your community. Be creative and make it fun. Once the money is raised, talk with some city officials or property owners to decide where the best place to plant the trees would be.

Be organized with your placement and don't be afraid to ask for help from your parents or youth leaders if you get hung up on something. Make the planting an event that all are invited to help with. Once the trees are planted, gather around with all those in attendance and read the story of creation from the book of Genesis (whatever translation you prefer).

sketch

PLEASE GO TO PAGE 6 FOR MORNING PRAYER

By the seventh day God had finished the work he had been doing; so on the seventh day he rested from all his work. And God blessed the seventh day and made it holy, because on it he rested from all the work of creating that he had done.

—GENESIS 2:2-3 (NIV)

In those days there was no king in Israel.
People did whatever they felt like doing.

—JUDGES 17:6 (THE MESSAGE)

broken

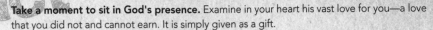

pray

THIS MORNING I PRAY…

Eternal God,

Help me to grasp the brokenness around me.

Help me to hear with my ears,

Touch with my hands, and see with my eyes

The images of separation from you that exist in this world.

I know that this will not be easy.

I know that this will not be fun.

But before light can come I must examine the darkness.

I must understand that it is real.

My prayer today and every day is simply

    that you would be near.

Amen

THIS DAY I PRAY…

Father God,

Create in me today a keen awareness for what is broken.

Be near as I examine the darkness

And breathe into me a mighty passion for change.

Amen

THIS NIGHT I PRAY…

My God, my God,

Now that I have seen, help me to believe

That though I have seen images of injustice,

    I can paint pictures of justice.

That though I have seen brokenness,

    I can strive for something restored.

That though I have been in darkness,

    I can live me life in the light.

This is my choice.

Amen

act

Take a moment to sit in God's presence. Examine in your heart his vast love for you—a love that you did not and cannot earn. It is simply given as a gift.

Say this to yourself: *My God is very fond of me. He takes delight in my very being.*

Broken Images. Take note of three images you observe today that remind you of the world's brokenness. Try to collect one having to do with the environment, one to do with relationships, and one to do with your community.

In the space below, title and describe the images you saw and address the emotions you feel while revisiting them in your mind.

pray

THIS MORNING I PRAY...

Help me to take interest in the paths
 of my brothers and sisters
Knowing that my lack of interest equals brokenness.
Help me to
 "learn to do right!
 Seek justice,
 Encourage the oppressed.
 Defend the cause of the fatherless,
 Plead the case of the widow."
 —Isaiah 1:17 (NIV)
In your name
Amen

THIS DAY I PRAY...

Father God,
Help me to listen as the blood of my brothers and sisters cries
 out from the ground.
Help me to know that I am my brother's keeper.
Amen

THIS NIGHT I PRAY...

Father God,
Forgive me for the hurt I have caused with my lack of interest
 for the protection and care of my brothers and sisters.
Help me always to be attentive to the blood crying out from
 the ground.
Help me always to own up to my mistakes instead of hiding
 behind my apathy.
I pray for the comfort of those who feel broken tonight.
For those who are tired, I pray for rest.
I thank you for your mercy.
Amen

act

Take Interest. Gather together with your creative community (if this is not possible, this activity can be done alone or with a partner). Read together the story of Cain and Abel. Afterwards, discuss Genesis 4:9, where Cain responds to God's query into the where-abouts of his brother by saying this: *Am I my brother's keeper?*

Instead of taking responsibility and owning up to the hurt he has caused his family and God, Cain chooses deceit and uninterest in the wake of his sin.

As a group, discuss the rhetorical question that Cain asks God. What is the answer?

Make a commitment to each other to take interest in something you know you have ignored for too long. Examples of this could be the person you never talk to because of the way that person acts, smells, or dresses; or the environmental action at home or on your campus that you simply have lacked the motivation to take. Maybe something else.

Choose one person to be your accountability partner, making sure you follow through. Let the story of Cain motivate you. Cain lacks the ability to give, becomes a murderer, and then lacks the ability to care in his attempt to ignore those he has hurt.

Before your group separates, pray together that you will not be like Cain but that you will take great interest in the care of your brothers and sisters. Report back to your accountability partner and document below some thoughts and feelings you have from this experience.

Bring reusable utensils to the school cafeteria for yourself and your friends. Make a habit of washing them and bringing them, or take turns as a group. This will reduce your waste of plastic ware.

sketch

pray

THIS MORNING I PRAY...

My God, my God,
Today I mourn for what is lost.
I examine the brokenness that is the product of my choice
To go my own way
To do my own thing
To separate myself from you.
In my prayers today I mourn this separation
Which is the product of my choice.
Amen

THIS DAY I PRAY...

My God, my God,
Help me to remember what is lost
And to properly mourn for what is broken.
I pray that I might never accept this
      broken state of things.
Amen

THIS NIGHT I PRAY...

My God, my God,
As I examine the dark and broken state of things,
I pray that I might always be about freeing the oppressed.
I pray that I might always be about taking the place
      of the down and out.
I pray that I might always be about relieving victims
      from the unfair circumstances.
Because I too have been oppressed, down and out,
      and a victim.
Give me the courage to bring remedy where
      there is only hurt.
Amen

act

Sit in God's presence once again this morning before you get ready for the day. As you sit, think about the fact that God is defined by love and that this love is so big that there is nowhere you can go to get away from it. Say to yourself: *My God is very fond of me. He takes delight in my very being.*

A pattern of brokenness that develops in the Bible when God's people turn away from him is slavery. Go online and collect some information on human slavery and human trafficking in the world today. Use the space below to jot down some of the statistics you find and also some of your thoughts and emotions as you encounter this global crisis. How does the act of slavery relate to brokenness?

You may think that this problem is a million miles away, but I bet it's closer than you think. Search for nearby organizations committed to putting an end to human trafficking and slavery in your community.

Make a commitment to visit their facilities and volunteer there at least once a week. This can be done with a friend or with your entire creative community.

Take some scissors and snip the rings of any six-pack holders you throw away in your home. Ask if you can do the same at your school so that fish, turtles, and other ocean animals with small necks don't get their heads stuck in these and choke.

sketch

pray

THIS MORNING I PRAY...

My God, my God,
I pray that I might reevaluate my needs,
That I might I see greed
    as not just a problem for the rich
But a problem for all of us broken people
Who think we need more than we actually do.
I pray that I might always be
    about feeding the hungry.
Amen

THIS DAY I PRAY...

My God, my God,
Help me to realize all that I have to give,
And help me to give it freely and joyfully.
Amen

THIS NIGHT I PRAY...

My God, my God,
As I examine the dark and broken state of things,
I pray that I might always be
    about feeding the hungry.
I pray that I might always be
    about taking the place of the down and out.
I pray that I might always be
    about relieving victims
    from unfair circumstances.
Because I too have been hungry and forgotten.
Give me the courage to bring remedy
    where there is only hurt.
Amen

act

Rest in God's amazing love for a moment. Think about how it is this great love that connects you very intimately with every single person. Say this to yourself: *My God is very fond of me. He takes delight in my very being.*

A food drive is when you collect nonperishable food items to give to the needy. So have one. The first step is to find a place to donate the food. This can be a rescue mission of some kind or a church with a homeless ministry. Usually these food drives are conducted with some sort of competition to see who can donate the most. You may decide to use this strategy on your campus or in your church.

Or you may decide to be a little more adventurous. Here are some ideas, or come up with your own. Have fun and remember: *the means are not as important as the mission.*

- Make it a literal food drive, declaring on your campus or in your church the day and time you will be driving through neighborhoods collecting food items. Blare the music and try not to get pulled over as you feed the hungry.

- Connect with a local movie theater and ask if you can set a date where ticket prices will be reduced for those who bring in a food item toward your cause.

- Connect with local artists and set up an art auction where the bidding is done with canned and boxed foods instead of money.

sketch

"The Serpent seduced me,"
she said, "and I ate."

—GENESIS 3:13

pray

THIS MORNING I PRAY...

My God, my God,
Be near as I examine the spirit of my rebellion.
Amen

THIS DAY I PRAY...

My God, my God,
Help me never to define you with rules
But instead to define you as a God who seeks relationship
Because this is the truth.
My rebellion, as big or small as it seems,
    changes things between us.
It pulls us apart.
It creates walls.
And so you hate it, and I must hate it too.
Help me to live my life walking toward you instead of away.
Amen

THIS NIGHT I PRAY...

My God, my God,
I pray that I might always put others before myself.
I realize that the core of my rebellion is selfishness.
This selfishness is the beast within me.
Telling me it's not that big a deal.
That it only affects me.
That it's only me.
Help me never to give in to this lie
And to always measure my decisions based on their effect
    upon my brothers and sisters.
I pray that I might always be about mending
    broken relationships.
Give me the courage to bring remedy where there
    is only hurt.
Amen

act

Rest in God's love. Think about the fact that though we have walked away from him, he has never stopped pursuing us. Say this to yourself: *My God is very fond of me. He takes delight in my very being.*

Rebel Effect. The most well-known act of rebellion in the Bible takes place with the fall of man, when Adam and Eve eat from the tree they have been told by God to stay away from. Eve is deceived by the serpent into thinking that eating from the tree is really not that big a deal; that, in fact, it will benefit her and Adam. The consequence of this sin is greater than they could ever have imagined.

This story is followed directly by the first murder, committed by Cain. So the rebellion of Adam and Eve not only creates broken relationship between God and man but also affects man's relationship with each other. Can you relate?

Use your sketch space on page 76 to write a story of your greatest rebellion, but do it from the perspective of someone else telling the story about you. You may even want to choose an individual to be your writing persona (a parent, a friend, a coach, a teacher, etc.).

Then ask yourself these questions:

What is at the heart of rebellion for you; where does it begin?

What were some of the consequences of this rebellious act that affected others?

Why do you believe God hates rebellion; what is at the heart of it for him?

 Carry a small towel in your bag that you can use in the restroom instead of paper towels. Encourage your friends to do the same.

sketch

pray

THIS MORNING I PRAY…

My God, my God,
This is my cry.
That I might never accept the kingdoms
    of the world
But instead always be striving for your kingdom
    to come.
Amen

THIS DAY I PRAY…

My God, my God,
Today I pray for sunlight.
I ask that, out of my community,
    you would raise a group of light-bearers…
Committed to your intentions for this world
    and your children.
Help us to be in our culture
    but not a product of our culture
Negotiating all our decisions in accordance
    to our relationship with you.
Open our eyes to the patterns of this world..
And help us to live outside of them
So that we might be an example for those
    who would look at us.
The way we act, talk, carry ourselves…
And see you.
Amen

THIS NIGHT I PRAY…

Prayer from page 6

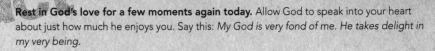

act

Rest in God's love for a few moments again today. Allow God to speak into your heart about just how much he enjoys you. Say this: *My God is very fond of me. He takes delight in my very being.*

Watch Television. For an hour sit down and watch some TV. But do it intentionally looking for attitudes of our culture that are the opposite of God's intended order of things. Try to pick out three things you see as contradictions of God's intentions for his creation. Document them in your sketch space, explaining your reasoning for each.

Afterwards, meet up with a friend to discuss these. Jot down some thoughts and emotions that come from your conversation. Here are a couple ideas to guide your discussion:

How does the pattern of sin that began with Adam and Eve still infect our culture today?

What are some of the negative effects of the attitudes you encountered in your hour of television?

How have these things affected you personally?

Do you know of local businesses that are not exercising good environmental practices? Make your voice heard. Take some time to write a letter and send it to them. You may think it's useless, but it's not. It is good for them to know that their irresponsibility is not going unnoticed.

sketch

PLEASE GO TO PAGE 6 FOR MORNING PRAYER

On the other hand, if they confess their sins and the sins of their ancestors, their treacherous betrayal, the defiance that set off my defiance that sent them off into enemy lands; if by some chance they soften their hard hearts and make amends for their sin, I'll remember my covenant with Jacob, I'll remember my covenant with Isaac, and, yes, I'll remember my covenant with Abraham. And I'll remember the land.

—LEVITICUS 26:40-42 (THE MESSAGE)

pray

THIS MORNING I PRAY…
Merciful God,
Forgive me my rebellious heart.
Turn me back to you.
Amen

THIS DAY I PRAY…
Merciful God,
Search my heart thoroughly.
Find the attitudes and habits within me
     that cause me to turn away.
I ask that you might break me of these things.
I confess them openly to you
In hopes that you will gather me under your wing
     like a mother hen.
Forgive me my rebellious heart and
     my transgression against you.
Amen

THIS NIGHT I PRAY…
Merciful God,
Forgive me of my missteps.
I pray that, among this vast corruption,
     you will find in me…
One who is righteous.
On who is blameless before you.
One who daily walks beside you.
I confess my sins and rest in your mercy
     forever and ever.
Amen

act

Pocket Confession. Think about your life. What is the greatest area of rebellion that you struggle with? Chances are, that something came to mind right away—maybe a couple things. Use the area below to depict this concern in your life. You can do this by actually writing it or writing a word that reminds you of it. You may want to draw a picture or symbol that signifies your rebellious habit.

Afterwards, cut or rip out the space and place the piece of paper in your pocket. Today as you walk around, each time you reach into your pocket and feel the piece of paper, pray a quick petition to God asking for forgiveness and then the strength to rid yourself of this behavior.

Use your sketch space to write or draw in response to the thoughts and emotions that have been revealed to you by doing this activity.

Clean out your car or your mom and dad's car. You would be surprised how much extra weight you carry in junk that could be removed. More weight means your car has to work harder to lug you around, which means lower gas mileage and higher fuel emissions.

sketch

pray

THIS MORNING I PRAY…

Forgive me for my selfishness.
Forgive me for my lack of care toward
my brothers and sisters.
Turn me back to you.
Amen

THIS DAY I PRAY…

Merciful God,
Search my heart thoroughly.
Today I confess my responsibility for
my brothers and sisters.
I pray that as I dwell within my community, you would
continually break my heart…
For the lost,
The hurting,
For the abused.
I pray that this passion would overcome
any other ambitions I may have,
Even if it means sacrifice.
Forgive my selfish spirit and
my transgressions against you.
Amen

THIS NIGHT I PRAY…

Forgive my missteps.
I pray that among this vast corruption,
you will find in me…
One who is righteous.
One who is blameless before you.
One who daily walks beside you.
I confess my sins and rest in your mercy forever and ever.
Amen

act

Campus Confessional. Gather together with your creative community and devise a plan to construct and facilitate a confessional booth on or near your campus. You may need to talk with school administrators to see if this is a possibility. If it is not, try to carry out your plan at a nearby location.

Once the location is decided and confirmed, gather the materials you will need. You can be as creative or uncreative as you like. You may be able to build an actual wood confessional (look online for examples), or you may have to settle for a couple tables with chairs. Regardless of the setup, the important thing is that you properly hype your confessional booth with dates and times of operation posted. If possible, you may want to set up your confessional booth at popular events in your community, or set up multiple locations with different people manning their designated booths and times.

While running your booth, here is what you will do— Usually at confessionals, it is the person entering who confesses and the person facilitating who listens. This will be the opposite. When people enter, explain to them that it is you who needs to confess for the following things (join with your creative community to construct a statement of confession if you wish):

Ask forgiveness for your inability to show them the true love of God and promise to do better.

Ask forgiveness for any hurt (through judging or other means) they might have been caused by the church or people claiming the Christian faith. Tell them you promise to do better.

Ask forgiveness for any time they have been in need and you were not there to help. Promise to do better.

You may add to this list, or write it out however you want. Make sure that your confession is sincere and gather together with your creative community afterwards to discuss reactions.

 Talk with your parents about starting a compost pile in your backyard. Make sure you do your research so you can maintain it correctly all by yourself.

pray

THIS MORNING I PRAY…

Merciful God,
Forgive me of my pride.
Help me to seek reconciliation
    wherever it is needed.
Turn me back to you.
Amen

THIS DAY I PRAY…

Merciful God,
Search my heart thoroughly.
Show me the walls that exist between
    me and my brothers and sisters.
Whether they are my doing or not…
Give me the humble spirit I need
    to destroy these barriers…
So you can be free to move among us
    and through us.
Forgive me my pride and my transgressions
    against you.
Amen

THIS NIGHT I PRAY…

Merciful God,
Forgive me of my missteps.
I pray that, among this vast corruption,
    you will find in me…
One who is righteous.
One who is blameless before you.
One who daily walks beside you.
I confess my sins and rest in your mercy
    forever and ever.
Amen

act

Make a List. Pray about this. Ask God to reveal to you certain relationships (names) from your past or present where a wound has been created and still remains. Make a list of these names and then proceed to seek these people out, asking forgiveness for your part in creating the problem. Don't expect anything in return; just make an honest and humble confession. Use the space below to jot down some of the thoughts and emotions you experience during this activity.

Do some research on the environmental problems at your school. How much waste is thrown out each day? How much Styrofoam and plastic? How much water is wasted? How much energy is used? Use this information to make informative signs and ask school administrators if you can hang them around school.

sketch

pray

THIS MORNING I PRAY...

Merciful God,
Forgive me my lustful heart.
Only you can give me my true identity.
Forgive me for looking elsewhere.
Turn me back to you.
Amen

THIS DAY I PRAY...

Merciful God,
Search my heart thoroughly.
How shamefully I beg for the comforts of this world.
How relentlessly I yearn after money and things.
I long to look a certain way in accordance with what I see.
In so many ways,
    I have been a slave to this media-driven world.
Show me how to be different.
Show me how to recognize the images
    of my culture as lies.
Forgive me my lust and my transgressions against you.
Amen

THIS NIGHT I PRAY...

Merciful God,
Forgive me of my missteps.
I pray that among this vast corruption,
    you will find in me
One who is righteous.
One who is blameless before you.
One who daily walks beside you.
I confess my sins and rest in your mercy
    forever and ever.
Amen

act

Burnt Confession Collage. Flip through some old magazines. Look for images inside that you feel drawn to. And address the question why. Why you feel drawn to that particular image? In some cases it may not be, but if you feel drawn to the image because it makes you want to look a certain way, act a certain way, have a certain kind of lifestyle, or own a certain thing, rip that image out.

When you have a handful of images, make some sort of collage with the pictures you collected. You can do this by pasting the images on a large poster board. Or you may want to simply staple the images together. You may feel the need to be more artistic with this, but have a reason behind each image in your collage.

Gather together with some friends from your creative community, possibly some who have created their own collages. Explain the collages and discuss the following questions:

How does it make you feel when you see such images?

What are some the dangers behind being drawn to such things?

How does this play into your relationship with God?

Afterwards confess to each other some of the struggles you have with longing after cultural images. Then burn your collages together. BE SAFE AND SMART, being sure to ask for assistance or permission if needed.

How often do you look at the backside of the cosmetics you buy to make sure they were made in a humane fashion with packaging that is completely recyclable? Make a habit of doing this and encourage your friends to do the same. Change brands if necessary. Some examples of companies that use inorganic or unsafe chemicals and/or test on animals are the following: L'Oreal, Clairol, Max Factor, Pantene, Suave, Johnson & Johnson, etc. Do your own research to determine which companies to support and which to avoid.

pray

THIS MORNING I PRAY...

Merciful God,

Forgive me for my lack of stewardship over this earth.

What a beautiful gift I have used as a doormat.

Forgive me.

Bring me back to you.

Amen

THIS DAY I PRAY...

Merciful God,

Search my heart thoroughly.

Show me ways that I can better care for creation

And give me the motivation to do so.

Help me to understand that caring for creation is not just a cool trend.

It is a vital part of returning to my intended purpose.

I am to be a caretaker.

A steward while the owner is away.

Forgive me for my lack of stewardship and my transgressions against you.

Amen

THIS NIGHT I PRAY...

Merciful God,

Forgive me for my missteps.

I pray that among this vast corruption, you will find in me

One who is righteous.

One who is blameless before you.

One who daily walks beside you.

I confess my sins and rest in your mercy forever and ever.

Amen

act

Operation Landfill. Visit your nearest landfill by yourself or with a friend. If you are not old enough to go alone, ask a parent or trusted mentor to go with you. Bring a piece of paper and pen, or use the space below, and jot down some of the thoughts and emotions you experience when you see how landfills operate. If you are with a partner, have a conversation afterwards about what you saw and write down some main points of your discussion.

Organize a no-trash day at your school. This will be a day when your whole school commits to no waste. Everything will either be reusable or 100% compostable. This day will hopefully inspire your campus to make lasting commitments to reducing waste.

sketch

pray

THIS MORNING I PRAY…

Merciful God,
I confess this morning my need to be broken.
I confess my need to be swept clean.
Bring me back to you.
Amen

THIS DAY I PRAY…

Merciful God,
Search my heart thoroughly.
Break me of all that is wicked in your sight.
Make a clean sweep.
Forgive me my transgressions against you.
Forgive me of my missteps.
I pray that among this vast corruption, you will find in me
One who is righteous.
One who is blameless before you.
One who daily walks beside you.
I confess my sin and rest in your mercy forever and ever.
Amen

THIS NIGHT I PRAY…

Prayer from page 6

act

Clean House. Clean your entire house today from top to bottom—a clean sweep. Even dig into the corners of your closet that have collected mold for far too long. Give your parents a break, and leave your abode spick and span. For those who are slightly more daring, make a surprise visit to the home of an elderly couple you know and volunteer to clean their home; maybe a grandparent or a friend from church.

Use your sketch space to respond with your thoughts on today's action. How did it feel? Did it hurt? Was it exhausting? How did it feel to be finished?

 **You hate cleaning for a reason.** Most household cleaning products are made from harmful chemicals that are not only bad for the environment but for you. But not to worry, you can make your own cleaning products from common household ingredients. Go online to research and complete this action.

sketch

PLEASE GO TO PAGE 6 FOR MORNING PRAYER

He waited seven more days and sent the dove out again, but this time it did not return to him. By the first day of the first month of Noah's six hundred and first year, the water had dried up from the earth. Noah then removed the covering from the ark and saw that the surface of the ground was dry. By the twenty-seventh day of the second month the earth was completely dry.

—GENESIS 8:12-14 (NIV)

pray

THIS MORNING I PRAY…

Creator God,

Your have cleaned the slate.

I believe it. Help me with my unbelief.

I pray that I can accept the mercy that you so freely give.

I thank you for your unlimited patience with me.

And I understand that there is a purpose behind it.

It's not so that I can continue carrying on
    the ways of old

But instead that I might be made a new creation,

A living and breathing portrait of your
    unbelievable mercy

So that people might see me and believe in you.

Amen

THIS DAY I PRAY…

Merciful God,

Thank you for never giving up on me.

Thank you for making my story a story of redemption.

Continue your patience with me, I pray.

Amen

THIS NIGHT I PRAY…

Father God,

As you have gently broken me

I pray that you will give me rest.

Help me rest in your commands

And use your instruction to build my life like a boat

That your mercy might be my bow

Guiding me in the midst of the wind and the waves.

Give me the confidence to accept the full portion
    of your mercy.

Every day.

Amen

act

Teaching a Child. Spend some time with a small child today. This should be a child you already know or whose parents know and trust you. Try and teach the child something new, or observe as her parents try to teach her something. Use the space below to document this as a psychologist might a case study, paying close attention to techniques and failed attempts.

After you have done so, use your notes to replay the situation in your mind. Think of a time when God has shown patience with you. What did you learn through that situation? In what way does your relationship with God resemble what you experienced with the child?

Use your sketch space to respond to this action.

Read by candlelight tonight instead of using electricity.

sketch

pray

THIS MORNING I PRAY…

Creator God,

Today I thank you for your unmerited protection

Though I have done nothing to deserve it.

You stand over me

Though I have done everything to hide myself away.

You never stop searching for me.

I pray that you might never stop the search.

That you would continually collect me from the
places I tend to get lost.

Amen

THIS DAY I PRAY…

Merciful God,

Thank you for never giving up on me.

Thank you for making my story one of grace.

In my brokenness, draw me close.

Amen

THIS NIGHT I PRAY…

Father God,

You see me at my worst and love anyhow.

I pray that my life might be lived in response
to your unmerited protection,

That, just as I have been shown mercy,

I would show mercy to others.

Thank you for not ending the story in the water.

Instead, you would not allow the flood to
sweep me away.

Give me the confidence to accept the
full portion of your mercy.

Every day.

Amen

act

After you pray, sit in God's mercy for a moment. Let it penetrate to the depths of your spirit, pulling out the things you feel the most shame about. Say this to yourself: *There is absolutely nothing I could do to make him love me less.*

Suggest that your family go together to the grocery store the next time it is needed. But instead of taking the car, walk. If it is too far, use public transportation. You will not only grow closer as a family, you will also be taking steps toward environmental awareness together.

There are many times in the Bible when God could have simply ended the story. After the fall and after the flood are two great examples of a God who provides mercy and protection when neither is deserved.

Can you think of someone in your life who has shown God to you in this way—providing second, third, fourth, etc., chances for you when you have done little to earn it? Write a short note of gratitude to this person today, explaining briefly how he or she has displayed God in your life.

sketch

The Lord God made garments of skin for Adam and his wife and clothed them.

—GENESIS 3:21 (NIV)

For as long as earth lasts, planting and harvest, cold and heat, summer and winter, day and night will never stop.

—GENESIS 8:22 (THE MESSAGE)

pray

THIS MORNING I PRAY...

Creator God,

I thank you today for the signs of your mercy
in nature.

This world is literally bursting with evidence
of your kingship.

The changing of the seasons.

The coming of a new day.

The quiet of the night.

In spite of my rebellion, you have blessed me
beyond my wildest imagination.

Amen

THIS DAY I PRAY...

Merciful God,

Thank you for never giving up on me.

Thank you for making my story one of beauty.

Help me to see this world as a gigantic picture of
your abundant mercy.

Amen

THIS NIGHT I PRAY...

Father God,

Thank you for all of this.

I look around and see shades of mercy everywhere.

I am surrounded by it.

The very turning of nature shows that you are
a God who heals wounds.

A god who redeems scars.

Give me the confidence to accept
the full portion of your mercy.

Every day.

Amen

act

Rest in God's mercy again this morning, thinking about God's inherent ability to bring life to dead places. Say this to yourself: *There is absolutely nothing I could do to make him love me less.*

Mercy's Season. Gather together with some friends from your creative community. Discuss in detail your favorite season or favorite time of day. In what way do you see God's mercy in the constant movement of nature? Use your sketch space to document your conversation and your thoughts.

sketch

pray

THIS MORNING I PRAY…

Creator God,
How awesome it is
That your mercy is made perfect in my weakness.
I say again: Your mercy is made perfect in my weakness.
I need not dress up for it.
I need not try to be someone else or something else.
Your mercy finds me just as I am,
At just the right time.
Amen

THIS DAY I PRAY…

Merciful God,
Thank you for never giving up on me.
Thank you for making my story one of rescue.
Help me never to doubt your plans for my life
    and this world.
Amen

THIS NIGHT I PRAY…

Father God,
You have come to my rescue.
You have pulled me from the depths.
You have extended your hand to me.
You have touched my leprous limbs and made them clean.
You have removed my sackcloth and placed me in robes.
Your have turned my weeping to dancing.
You have calmed the waters of my soul.
You have done all this because you love me.
Oh how you love me.
I accept your mercy.
Amen

act

Story of Rescue. Gather together with your creative community and split up into teams (twos, threes, fours, whatever works). The task of each team will be to think up/write/ illustrate a story. The theme of this story should be rescue.

After all the stories are created, gather together and have each team tell its story about rescue to the group. Afterwards discuss this:

How many of the stories have a point where all seems lost? Why do we associate this kind of timing with stories of rescue? Think of the movies or books that you love… Same thing, right?

What if it is because the story of this world is one where all seemed lost and then mercy came to our rescue just in time?

What if we made it a habit to create these kind of stories within our community and our world?

As a group, discuss some situations you know of where all seems lost. *What can be done to bring rescue?*

 Do some research and make sure you are protecting your garden with the most eco-friendly pesticides available.

sketch

Then Noah built an altar to the Lord and, taking some of all the clean animals and clean birds, he sacrificed burnt offerings on it. The Lord smelled the pleasing aroma and said in his heart: Never again will I curse the ground because of man, even though every inclination of his heart is evil from childhood. And never again will I destroy all living creatures, as I have done.

—GENESIS 8:20-21 (THE MESSAGE)

pray

THIS MORNING I PRAY…
Creator God,
You have remembered me in my brokenness.
Even though I am unworthy…
I have been given a place at the table.
I have been invited and I accept.
Amen

THIS DAY I PRAY…
Merciful God,
Thank you for never giving up on me.
Thank you for making my story
　　one of prayers heard.
I pray that my life would be an altar
　　reminding others of your mercy.
Amen

THIS NIGHT I PRAY…
Father God,
Though every inclination of my heart is wicked,
You have given me your word that
　　you will never forget me.
There are no words to express how cool that is.
Please accept my feeble displays as
　　gratitude for your infinite mercy.
Give me the confidence to accept
　　the full portion.
Every day.
Amen

act

Rest in his mercy. What can you do in response to such a wonderful thing? Say this: *There is absolutely nothing I could do to make him love me less.*

To the Table. Here are some options that can be done alone or with a group: Build a table. Nothing fancy—just four legs and a base of any size, or purchase a table from a secondhand store (don't spend more than ten bucks), or rescue and restore one from the Dumpster.

Then…decorate it with images, words, scribbles, whatever reminds you of God's mercy in your life.

Then…place the table in a prominent place in your life. If you did this alone, you may want it in your bedroom (more conducive to small tables). If you did it with friends, you may want it in your youth room at church or a place where you all hang out, like a friend's basement.

When Noah emerges from the ark on Mount Ararat, he immediately builds an altar to show his eternal gratitude to God for the mercy shown to him and his family. They have made it through the flood.

Use your sketch space to respond about some of your thoughts on this activity.

Make a list of the vegetables your parents usually buy from the grocery store and let them know that you will be making a trip to the local farmers' market to purchase them.

sketch

pray

THIS MORNING I PRAY…
Creator God,
Help me master the skill of accepting your mercy.
Amen

THIS DAY I PRAY…
Merciful God,
Thank you for never giving up on me.
Thank you for making my story
    a story of undeniable mercy.
Amen

THIS NIGHT I PRAY…
Prayer from page 6

Rainbows of Mercy. As a sign of God's covenant with Noah, he places a rainbow in the sky as a visible reminder of his infinite mercy for his fallen children. In what way is your life consistently displaying God's mercy every day?

Pray about it. And use the space below to make a covenant with God about the three things you will do every day to show mercy to others around the world, in your community, in your family, etc.

Take a picture of nature with your phone or with a camera. If you don't have one, maybe you can borrow a camera from a friend. Make this picture the background on your desktop, background on your phone, or tape it to your dashboard as a reminder of God's gifts to you.

sketch

PLEASE GO TO PAGE 6 FOR MORNING PRAYER

Give in to God, come to terms with him and everything will turn out just fine. Let him tell you what to do; take his words to heart. Come back to God Almighty and he'll rebuild your life. Clean house of everything evil. Relax your grip on your money and abandon your gold-plated luxury. God Almighty will be your treasure, more wealth than you can imagine.

—JOB 22:21 (THE MESSAGE)

pray

THIS MORNING I PRAY…

Sustainer God,

Help me examine the unneeded things in my life.

As I enter into this new covenant with you,
    I pray that I can clear space.

Enough space for you to move about freely.

Forgive me for mucking up the waters for so long.

Help me to rely on your provision more than
    anything or anyone.

I commit this week to fasting and removing the
    obstacles between us.

Amen

THIS DAY I PRAY…

Creator God,

I realize that in this broken state, there are barriers
    between us.

These things separating us are my fault.

Forgive me.

Use this week of fasting and prayer to clean house

So that you can reside within.

Amen

THIS NIGHT I PRAY…

Father God,

Your promise is that you would preserve creation.

And yet I make every effort to preserve myself.

Help me believe that you are all I need.

Grab hold of my passions and desires.

So that you might be all that I want as well.

Amen

act

Empty Closets. Go to your closet and examine all the clothes you have. As you are doing this, begin to pull out all the clothes you never wear. Fold these up and place them in a laundry basket. How much is left? Is it more than you actually need? Pray about this and be honest with yourself. Pull out all that you feel is unnecessary and fold it up, placing it with the rest of the excess clothing.

Donate the clothing to a local homeless shelter or a nearby organization that distributes clothes to those in need.

As an extended project, join with your creative community to have a clothing drive on your campus. Use any means of marketing available to you to ask the students on your campus to clean out their closets, bringing the clothes to a certain place of your designation. Be creative and efficient with how you do this and make sure all the collected clothing gets to the proper charities.

Make a commitment to eating more plant-based food. I'm not saying become a vegetarian, although it is okay if you are. The balance of the world's diet is heavily weighted on the side of meat and dairy. This results in the flourishing of large-scale livestock production, which has been proven to be very hard on the earth. Having a more plant-centered diet might help balance the scales.

sketch

act

Fast a meal each day of this week. There are many reasons why it is important to do this, none of which have anything to do with trying to lose weight. Fasting is strictly a religious observance created by the act of abstaining. What we observe is God's ultimate provision—his ability to sustain us physically, spiritually, and emotionally.

While you fast you will feel hungry, and in your hunger, pray. This is not some sort of contract binding God to answer your prayers. It is an outward expression of your reliance on God over the things of this world, including food.

Today, as you fast, think and pray on this:

Think of all that you have, compared to so many in the world who have close to nothing. Pray that God will redefine what you believe you need to sustain life.

pray

THIS MORNING I PRAY...

Sustainer God,
I pray that my life would be about giving good gifts
As you are about giving good gifts.
I pray that as I sacrifice my life to you
I would learn to always give my best.
My first fruits.
May the gifts I give and the sacrifices I make
Be a pleasing aroma for you.
Amen

THIS DAY I PRAY...

Creator God,
I give my best to you,
Because my best is what you require.
And because you have given your best to me
Freely.
Because you have given freely, so I freely give.
Amen

THIS NIGHT I PRAY...

Father God,
Help me to understand what it means to sacrifice my best.
Help my giving to be an outpouring of my gratitude to
     you.
I pray that I might never become so attached to
     material things
That I am not ready to give them up in a second for you.
By giving you my best, I remove myself from the patterns
     of this world.
And enter into complete reliance on your provision.
Your portion is sufficient.
It is all I need.
I pray not to be divided but to be wholly yours.
Amen

act

As you fast a meal today, think and pray about this: Do you segment your life into spiritual and non-spiritual? For example, basketball practice after school is non-spiritual and Wednesday night church is obviously spiritual. What if you made a habit of devoting all your life and time to God, no matter what that meant?

This might mean giving up some things or adding some things. It might mean changing your routine. In prayer, sacrifice your time to God completely, asking the Holy Spirit to reside in all the nooks and crannies of your lifestyle.

Offering. Give a good gift today. Simple as that. Think of something within your possession that you feel someone else might really enjoy or need and give it freely—no strings attached. This may be something you will miss a great deal. Pray about your decision and that God would bless your sacrifice. Use your sketch space to respond to your thoughts and emotions.

As a class gift to your school, recommend that you plant an organic vegetable garden on the grounds for the cafeteria.

sketch

THIS MORNING I PRAY…
Sustainer God,
I know that there are things in my life
That remove me from your provision.
As I fast, help me to remove myself from these things.
I place them at your feet.
Amen

THIS DAY I PRAY…
Creator God,
I pray that whenever things get out of hand
Whenever something possesses too much of me
And there is a need for change
You would return me to the water
Where I can start again.
Fresh.
This is what I need today.
Amen

THIS NIGHT I PRAY…
Father God,
I pray that when things seem out of hand
Overwhelming
Out of control
I would rest within capable hands.
Tear into these layers of useless skin
    I have created around me
And help me to focus only on what is true and good.
Amen

As you fast a meal today, think and pray about this: Pray that God will show you something in your life that has to go—some behavior, attitude, habit, or addiction that you know has plagued you for far too long. What is keeping you from stepping away from this behavior? Do you believe that you can rely on God to beat this problem once and for all?

40-Day Flood. Mark 40 days out on your calendar and spend those 40 days abstaining from the behavior, attitude, habit, or addiction you felt God bringing to the forefront in your fasting and praying today. Of course, the hope is that you can abstain for good, but commit to this 40 days as an intentional change in your pattern of life. Mark off the days one by one so you can reflect on how God is slowly changing you. This is a big step in clearing space and removing obstacles.

 Check all the faucets and pipes in your house today for leaks. Make a habit of doing this periodically. You would be surprised how much water is wasted every day because of just one dripping pipe.

act

Today, as you fast and pray, think on this:

Then God blessed Noah and his sons, saying to them,
"Be fruitful and increase in number and fill the earth.
The fear and dread of you will fall upon all the beasts of the earth
and all the birds of the air, upon every creature that moves along the ground,
and upon all the fish of the sea; they are given into your hands.
Everything that lives and moves will be food for you.
Just as I gave you the green plants, I now give you everything."

—GENESIS 9:1-3 (NIV)

pray

THIS MORNING I PRAY…
Sustainer God,
I pray this morning for a clear and focused vision.
Amen

THIS DAY I PRAY…
Creator God,
How easily my eyes stray away from your purpose.
How shameful are the deviations of my heart and mind.
As I fast and pray, remind me, Father
In my life, relationships, and in my community.
Remind me of the original vision.
Forgive me for trying to make it something it's not.
Amen

THIS NIGHT I PRAY…
Father God,
I commit myself to the substance of life again.
Help me to always be about collecting
    the stories of others.
Helping them when they need help.
I realized that the plans I make without you are
    formless and empty.
Yet the plans I make within your intentions are
    able to penetrate the deepest darkness
And mend the greatest wounds.
Instead of navigating in a dense fog, help me
    to begin to see like you.
To rest in your promises.
And to carry out your purposes.
In my life, my relationships, and my community.
Amen

act

In the ninth chapter of Genesis, God gives Noah a clear and focused purpose for mankind: *Bring substance to the world and take care of everything in it.* By the eleventh chapter, men have decided to steer a different direction. They have decided to do their own thing and build a city and a tower that God never intended. So God scatters them and returns to the drawing board.

Refocus. Gather together with your creative community. When you began this group, it was for one purpose and one purpose only. Do you remember what it was? Discuss this with your group and establish a plan to return to the original intent of your meeting. This might mean you publicize the group again, trying to recruit new participants.

After your discussion, use this week to organize a day of community service. This will be a day where you and your friends go into the community to care for those who have a need. Keep your ears open for opportunities and pick a few needs that you feel your group can remedy. Pray together that this time will be for refreshing and refocusing your group.

sketch

act

In the book *The Voyage of the Dawn Treader*, from *The Chronicles of Narnia* series by C.S. Lewis, there is a boy named Eustace. And Eustace is simply a mess. His attitude is bad. He's selfish. He is a terror to deal with and, in short, a broken young child badly in need of change.

Through an interesting turn of events, Eustace becomes a dragon, and his time as a dragon makes him realize the error of his ways. One day, in what he thinks might have been a dream, Eustace meets the great lion Aslan.

The two stand alongside a refreshingly wonderful-looking spring. Eustace longs to take a swim, yet Aslan tells him he must remove his dragon skin in order to do so.

Despite Eustace's best efforts, he can't remove all of his scaly layers. So Aslan asks if he would like for him to try. Eustace submits, and Aslan tears away at the thick dragon skin. It hurts like crazy, but Eustace is soon swimming in the cool and refreshing spring with skin that seems brand new.

Use the extra sketch pages in the back of the book to write down some thoughts or a story of how the tale of Eustace applies to your life.

Then, thinking about your story, grab some crayons or colored pencils and draw a dragon with multiple layers. You may want to label each layer with a certain attitude or habit from which God has delivered you. You may want to just think of these things in your head as you color each layer.

Sometimes remembering where we came from refreshes our hope for further change.

pray

THIS MORNING I PRAY…
Sustainer God,
Help me to understand and embrace
the idea of clearing space.
Fasting is not fun,
but I don't do it with a negative spirit.
I don't do it believing it's punishment.
I do it because I believe your promises are
better that the promises of this world.
When I rely on the promises of this world,
things get broken.
And I long for more.
I long to emerge from the rubble and
take hold of your promise.
But first I must be stripped down
to my baby skin.
I understand.
And I pray that it would be so.
Amen

THIS DAY I PRAY…
Creator God,
Prepare me.
Prepare me.
Prepare me.
Amen

THIS NIGHT I PRAY…
Father God,
I submit myself to your claws.
I understand it may hurt.
But I long for new skin.
Amen

act

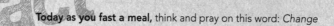

Today as you fast a meal, think and pray on this word: *Change*

Does your house receive a lot of junk mail or mail-order catalogs that never get looked at?
Take the time to call these businesses before you dispose of the mailings and ask personally to be removed from their lists. This will cut down on their costs of printing and the waste that occurs when these get thrown away. Even if you recycle them, it will save money if they never have to be printed in the first place.

sketch

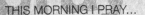

pray

THIS MORNING I PRAY…
Sustainer God,
I have a history of brokenness.
Yet you continually heal me.
I have a history of getting lost within myself.
Yet you always come and drag me out.
I have a history of being fickle in my faith.
Yet you are always taking me back.
I have a history of breaking promises.
Yet you are always keeping yours.
My prayer is that you would do it again.
Amen

THIS DAY I PRAY…
Prepare me for your promise.
Amen

THIS NIGHT I PRAY…
Prayer from page 6

act

Preparations. Use the space below to write down some things God has shown you through your fasting. Then gather together with your creative community and have a huge meal. Have everyone bring his or her favorite food and enjoy!

 Simplify meals by making more. Talk with your family about preparing large portions that will leave leftovers that can be stored. This will reduce cooking time and assure your family the most efficient use of kitchen ingredients.

sketch

Give in to God, come to terms with him and everything will turn out just fine. Let him tell you what to do; take his words to heart. Come back to God Almighty and he'll rebuild your life. Clean house of everything evil. Relax your grip on your money and abandon your gold-plated luxury. God Almighty will be your treasure, more wealth than you can imagine.

—JOB 22:21 (THE MESSAGE)

After this, the word of the Lord came to Abram in a vision: "Do not be afraid, Abram. I am your shield, your very great reward."

—GENESIS 15:1 (NIV)

Abram believed the Lord, and he credited it to him as righteousness.

—GENESIS 15:6 (NIV)

promise

pray

act

THIS MORNING I PRAY...

Father God,

How generous you are to me.

You have prepared me a house before I even
thought to gather the wood to build one.

You have led me to the door when I thought myself
content to wander in the cold.

You have made me a promise.

I pray that I may have the kind of faith that will have
you call me righteous.

Amen

THIS DAY I PRAY...

Father God,

I believe.

Help me with my unbelief.

Amen

THIS NIGHT I PRAY...

Father God,

Here I am, listening.

Forgive me for having a faith that is rational.

Help me to believe the unbelievable.

After all, nothing is too hard for you.

Amen

Irrational Faith. With Abraham, God begins the work of restoring his people with a promise—an unbelievable one. Abraham is old, and his wife is barren, and yet God tells him that he will raise a great nation from his offspring. Unbelievably, he believes, and then it happens. Is your faith practical? In your sketch space, include some situations in your life where it would be unbelievable for God to make a difference. Pray and believe. Watch what happens.

Sometimes being environmentally conscious can seem like a lost cause. I mean, how much difference can one person really make by being green? Well, the truth is, not much. One person—alone—can't accomplish change unless that person influences others to do likewise. Think about what you can do to inspire others to be better stewards.

sketch

pray

THIS MORNING I PRAY…

Father God,
You have set your plan in motion.
Long before I could understand, you were making
    preparations for me.
Thank you, Father.
You have looked on me with great concern
And longed for my safekeeping.
Amen

Option: During your prayer time, read Isaiah 43:1-3.

THIS DAY I PRAY…

Father God,
You are a great God.
You keep your promises.
Amen

THIS NIGHT I PRAY…

Father God,
What a perfect picture!
Every breath I breathe, every misstep, every promise,
It is all leading to the cross.
You have made it so, and I thank you.
Amen

act

Big Picture Promise. Join together with your creative community. Gather some painting and drawing supplies. Paint or construct a large cross with open space inside. As a group, use the inside of the cross to paint/draw/write words and pictures that depict God's promise in your life. Everything inside the cross. Pray together.

Paint can release toxins into the air for years after application. But there is non-toxic paint you can buy that is much less dangerous for the environment.

pray

THIS MORNING I PRAY...

Father God,
I praise you for the struggle,
For it is in the struggles
That I hold onto your promise
All the more.
Amen

THIS DAY I PRAY...

Father God,
I believe that you are good
All the time
And in all things.
Amen

THIS NIGHT I PRAY...

Father God,
I pray that in the struggle,
I will draw closer and closer to you.
Use these times of trouble to craft me
   into the person
You dream for me to be.
Amen

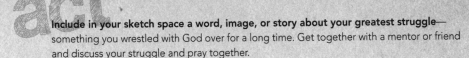

act

Include in your sketch space a word, image, or story about your greatest struggle— something you wrestled with God over for a long time. Get together with a mentor or friend and discuss your struggle and pray together.

Work in the garden today. Creating a healthy, organic vegetable garden is not only hard physical work. Proper research is required to know what you're doing. Are you embracing the struggle?

sketch

pray

THIS MORNING I PRAY...

Father God,
I am yours.
You have made me your treasured possession.
You have spared me with compassion,
Like a loving father would show
    his son or daughter.
You have set me apart.
Amen

THIS DAY I PRAY...

Father God,
I believe that in me you have found great joy.
Help me with my unbelief.
Amen

THIS NIGHT I PRAY...

Father God,
You are my shepherd,
And I am your prized sheep.
You have delivered me from trouble
And blessed me beyond what I deserve.
May your name be echoed in me.
May the sound cover the earth.
Amen

act

Write this on 10 pieces of paper: *You are God's treasured possession.* Make those 10 pieces of paper into 10 paper airplanes. If you don't know how, ask for help. Float those 10 paper airplanes at 10 unsuspecting people. It might spark an interesting conversation. Include in your sketch space your airplane interactions.

 Talk with administrators at your school about making recycle bins for paper just as accessible as regular trashcans. The goal would be to operate under a one-for-one policy—meaning that for every trashcan there is also a recycle bin.

sketch

pray

THIS MORNING I PRAY...

Father God,
I lift my eyes to the hills.
Where does my help come from?
My help comes from the Lord,
The maker of heaven and earth.
He will not let my foot slip.
Amen

THIS DAY I PRAY...

He who watches over me will not slumber;
Indeed, he who watches over Israel
Will neither slumber nor sleep.
The Lord watches over me—
The Lord is my shade at my right hand.
Amen

THIS NIGHT I PRAY...

The sun will not harm me by day,
Nor the moon by night.
The Lord will keep me from all harm—
He will watch over my life;
The Lord will watch over my coming and going
Both now and forevermore.
Amen

act

Go online and listen to any version you can find of the old hymn "Be Still, My Soul." This might not be your kind of music, but as you listen, concentrate on the lyrics. Include in your sketch space a reaction in pictures or words.

Organize a "lights out" block party. This would be an event where everyone in your neighborhood refrains from the use of electricity in their homes for one evening and comes outside to hang out. Be creative and make this a fun thing that people will want to do again.

sketch

Be still, my soul: the Lord is on thy side. Bear patiently the cross of grief or pain.

Leave to thy God to order and provide; In every change, he faithful will remain.

Be still, my soul: thy best, thy heavenly Friend. Through thorny ways leads to a joyful end.

Be still, my soul: thy God doth undertake. To guide the future, as he has the past.

Thy hope, thy confidence let nothing shake; All now mysterious shall be bright at last.

Be still, my soul: the waves and winds still know. His voice who ruled them while he dwelt below.

Be still, my soul: the hour is hastening on. When we shall be forever with the Lord.

When disappointment, grief, and fear are gone, Sorrow forgot, love's purest joys restored.

Be still, my soul: when change and tears are past

All safe and blessed, we shall meet at last.

(*SING TO THE LORD*/HYMN 97, LILLENAS PUBLISHING)

pray

THIS MORNING I PRAY...
Father God,
You are the "I AM"
A hero to those who believe and obey
Because of your promise.
I am not alone to fight my battles.
I am taken care of
Forever and ever.
Amen

THIS DAY I PRAY...
Father God,
I believe that you have always come to my rescue,
And I believe you always will.
Help me with my unbelief.
Amen

THIS NIGHT I PRAY...
Prayer from pg. 6

act

In your sketch space today, reflect on the word *hero* with images and words.

Reflect on how these words go together:

Hero and Power

Hero and Rest

Hero and Promise

Hero and God

Check out the roofs of the businesses in your town. What color are they? Black roofs absorb heat so that it takes more energy to cool the inside. Simply painting roofs white would reflect the heat away and not only lower energy bills but conserve energy too. Local business owners might be interested in that, so let them know.

sketch

PLEASE GO TO PAGE 6 FOR MORNING PRAYER

sketch

promise 07

pray

THIS MORNING I PRAY…
Father God,
Lead me to your table.
You have set me apart.
I pray that all that is inside me
Might be genuine to your seal.
Amen

THIS DAY I PRAY…
Father God,
You have drawn me out,
Released me from captivity.
You have saved my soul
Because you love me.
Amen

THIS NIGHT I PRAY…
Father God,
Help me to always remember
How you heard my cry
And delivered me.
Amen

act

Get together with your creative community and some of your spiritual mentors and organize a Seder meal to celebrate the Passover. Invite your friends and family to participate in this with you. Also, make it open to anyone who wants to join.

Make it a family practice to prepare one-pot meals. This will not only save time but energy, and you might just stumble across a mixing of ingredients that becomes a family favorite.

sketch

pray

THIS MORNING I PRAY…

Father God,
You have prepared for me a way out
Of the messes I create.
When I deserved your wrath,
You demonstrated your love
And put another in my place.
Amen

THIS DAY I PRAY…

Father God,
Help me to accept your mercy.
Place it like a seal over my heart.
Amen

THIS NIGHT I PRAY…

Father God,
I worship you tonight, Jehovah Jireh,
    my provider.
In my place, you have placed a lamb.
And because of that I am free
To lived a blessed life,
Free from guilt or condemnation.
Help me to live out your example
With mercy and grace.
Amen

act

Read Exodus 12:1-13. Use your sketch space to draw depictions of each step in the preparation of the Passover meal. Don't worry if your drawings are bad. When you are finished, think about the importance of each step. How is God setting up what is to come? Discuss this with a friend, parent, or mentor.

Research the steps to proper composting then take steps to involve your community. This might mean having neighborhood-wide compost or maybe even asking city officials about the possibility of a municipal compost system.

sketch

pray

THIS MORNING I PRAY...
Father God,
Help me to live within your laws,
Not because I have to—
You wouldn't care for that—
Instead, as an outpouring of my thankful spirit,
In response to the outpouring of your Spirit to me.
Amen

THIS DAY I PRAY...
Father God,
Help me accept your commandments
As the guidelines of my life.
Make them like a seal over my heart.
Amen

THIS NIGHT I PRAY...
In your unfailing love, you will lead
The people you have redeemed.
In your strength you will guide them
To your holy dwelling.
(Exodus 15:13)

act

Join together with your creative community. Bring your Bibles and list out the Ten Commandments as a group. Discuss God's purpose behind each. Some will be obvious (do not kill, commit adultery, steal), but attempt to go deeper than the surface answer. Make a commitment this week to display each commandment in your life in some way and use your sketch space to document your experiences.

Join together with your creative community and come up with ten commandments of environmental awareness in the classroom. Ask school administrators if these can be posted in prominent places for all to see (maybe even every class).

sketch

pray

THIS MORNING I PRAY…

Father God,
Help us to live as people of promise
So that people might see our good deeds
And believe in you.
Amen

THIS DAY I PRAY…

Father God,
Help me reveal your promise to others
With the works that you lead me to do.
May it be like a seal over my heart.
Amen

THIS NIGHT I PRAY…

Father God,
I pray that your love might be revealed in my actions.
Amen

act

Use your sketch space to draw some images that come to mind when you think about being set apart. What does that mean in your life? Being a child of promise is not just an inward thing. It is displayed in our acts. Today, pick out 10 people you can do something for to make their lives better. Use your sketch space to jot down the names (if you know them; if not, find out) and what you intend to do to help.

What other ideas do you have to make your school greener? Use the rest of your sketch space to jot down these ideas and start to dream of ways to make it happen. Don't be afraid to be bold when you see something and have a vision to make it better.

sketch

pray

THIS MORNING I PRAY…

Father God,
As your chosen child,
You have provided all that I need.
I pray that I might accept your portion
And be filled.
Amen

THIS DAY I PRAY…

Father God,
Forgive me for seeking satisfaction elsewhere.
Help me to think of others before myself
And be filled by your provisions in my life,
Like a seal upon my heart.
Amen

THIS NIGHT I PRAY…

Father God,
Help me to give recklessly
To those who are in great need.
Help me to do all I can
    to undo the imbalances
That exist all around me.
Help me to live on simply enough.
Amen

act

When God's people set out across the desert from Egypt to the promised land, they are provided food from heaven called manna. God gives equally, and everyone has just enough for each day. This is to be their portion, yet eventually they long for more. God's intention is for his people to live simply and trust. In your sketch space, list some things you can do to live more simply in your consumption of resources. Also, list some ways you can give out of your abundance to those who don't have as much.

 **Talk with your family about using household appliances less often, or even not at all.** Discuss ideas on how to do this. Here are some suggestions: hang clothes to dry, only wash full loads (of both dishes and clothes), or have a set time limit to all showers.

sketch

pray

THIS MORNING I PRAY…
Father God,
You have promised
That you would never leave me in bondage,
That when I cry out you would always hear
And come to my altar.
Help me to do the same for those enslaved.
Amen

THIS DAY I PRAY…
Father God,
Open my eyes to the slaves around me.
Plant in me a great longing for their freedom
Like a seal upon my heart.
Amen

THIS NIGHT I PRAY…
Prayer from page 6

act

What things can you think of that people become enslaved by? As the story of God's children progresses, we find that God, over and over again, will go to any length to save his people from the things that trap them. This is part of his amazing promise. Are you living out that promise in your life? Today, think of a way to come beside someone you know who is enslaved by things like addiction, abusive relationships, depression, etc. What would it look like for you to join this person in his or her struggle?

 What usually keeps people from being more environmentally conscious is an addiction to convenience. It's convenient to buy vegetables from the grocery. It's convenient to throw everything in the trashcan. Use your sketch space to list some things that show your addiction to convenience. How can you remedy this?

sketch

PLEASE GO TO PAGE 6 FOR MORNING PRAYER

On the other hand, if they confess their sins and the sins of their ancestors, their treacherous betrayal, the defiance that set off my defiance that sent them off into enemy lands; if by some chance they soften their hard hearts and make amends for their sin, I'll remember my covenant with Jacob, I'll remember my covenant with Isaac, and, yes, I'll remember my covenant with Abraham. And I'll remember the land.

—LEVITICUS 26:40-42 (THE MESSAGE)

pray

THIS MORNING I PRAY...
God my King,
Forgive me for allowing this world to name me
When only you are able.
Forgive me for relenting your throne to the
    things of this world.
I declare you again as King over my life.
Amen

THIS DAY I PRAY...
God my King,
I pray that I will only find my identity in you.
Give me the strength to toss aside the other things.
Forgive me for allowing them to rule my life.
Amen

THIS NIGHT I PRAY...
God my King,
You have made me a promise,
That you would rule over my life
With love, justice, and mercy.
But I must submit to your authority.
There is no one like you.
I am forever the lion cub.
Amen

act

FTLC. Today, after your prayer, wait for a moment. Picture this in your mind: You are a lion cub lounging against the large chest of your father (imagine Mufasa from the *Lion King,* or Aslan from *Narnia*). Let this image sink in for a moment. Use your sketch space to jot down some images or words that fill your mind. As you go through this day, list out all the things that keep you from remaining within the paws of your father. Here are a few things to think about—cliques, fashion, expectations, peer pressure, etc.

 Take a break from the car. This might mean riding a bike or maybe even the bus. Embrace the experience. Look around. Pay attention to faces and listen for stories. Use your remaining sketch space to document what happens.

sketch

pray

THIS MORNING I PRAY...
Father God,
You have done great things.
Though I have strayed...
You have always taken my side...
In times of struggle and hardship.
Help me never to forget.
Amen

THIS DAY I PRAY...
Father God,
Thank you for these stories.
They help me to remember.
Amen

THIS NIGHT I PRAY...
God, my King,
You defeated Goliath with a rock and a sling.
You made Jericho into rubble with
    the marching of feet
And the sounds of the trumpets.
You can, assuredly, take care of me.
Amen

act

STORY TIME. Gather together with your creative community. Have a time of storytelling where you all share an example of the beauty of God's authority and power in your life as you have gone through this experience. Include in your sketch space some images or words that come to mind as you listen and share yourself.

 In case you haven't already, change out all your light bulbs for energy-efficient bulbs.

sketch

David said, "I've been a shepherd, tending sheep for my father. Whenever a lion or bear came and took a lamb from the flock, I'd go after it, knock it down, and rescue the lamb. If it turned on me, I'd grab it by the throat, wring its neck, and kill it. Lion or bear, it made no difference—I killed it. And I'll do the same to this Philistine pig who is taunting the troops of God-Alive. God, who delivered me from the teeth of the lion and the claws of the bear, will deliver me from this Philistine." Saul said, "Go. And God help you!"

—1 SAMUEL 17:34 (THE MESSAGE)

pray

THIS MORNING I PRAY...

Father God,
Help me to see and understand the consequences
Of our disobedience.
We have turned from you, and it has caused
Hurt, heartache, brokenness, scars.
But every day I have a choice.
I pray that I might renew my promise to you
To take care of this earth and all its creatures.
Amen

THIS DAY I PRAY...

God, my King,
Oh, how you love us.
Oh, how you long to redeem the scars
That we have created.
Help us to bring about change.
Amen

THIS NIGHT I PRAY...

Father God,
I pray for those
Who are badly in need of renewed hope.
Turn us toward their cries.
Help us never to give up the search
For those who are lost and broken,
As you have never given up the search
For us.
Amen

act

Gathering Change. Meet with your creative community. Decide on a cause you all feel adamant about giving to. Spend some time praying together about this cause, especially focusing on the need for forgiveness due to the disobedience that has caused it. Find some sort of large container and decorate it as a group. Find a place in your community—school, youth room, church—where you can have a place for donations to be accepted continually in the container. Be responsible, and make sure the money always gets in the right hands.

Do some research on the World Wildlife Fund (*www.worldwildlifefund.org*). How can you and your group get involved in their mission to save wildlife? Maybe it's just by donating and wearing a t-shirt. Maybe it's more than that.

pray

THIS MORNING I PRAY…

Father God,
You are my unmoving stone,
My foundation and fortress.
I run to you to save me,
And I am saved.
I will sing songs of praise
Forever.
Amen

THIS DAY I PRAY…

Father God,
Make me a "singer of songs"
In my ups and downs.
Help me to always find ways to praise you.
Amen

THIS NIGHT I PRAY…

Father God,
I lay my life at your feet,
All these jagged pieces.
And I pray that you would bring them together.
Tune me to the ways of your heart.
Help me not to miss a thing.
You have taken great interest in my life
And given it color.
So I will sing to you.
Amen

A Singer of Songs. Spend some time this week with the story of King David. Peruse the books of 1 and 2 Samuel and 1 and 2 Kings to learn about life. Include in your sketch space some words that you feel define his life. David makes some poor decisions in his life that come with major consequences. Yet at the end, he is considered a man after God's own heart and a "singer of songs" that bring praise to God. Today, begin the habit of writing songs of praise to God. It doesn't matter if you are musically inclined or good with words. This is just between you and God anyway. Find a place, with each written lyric, where you can sing or say the words aloud. Hold this time close to your heart, knowing that God does as well.

 Adopt a "spot" in nature. This might be the place you go to sing your songs, pray, or just to be among creation. Every time you go there, take a tote to pick up trash. This will strengthen your connection with your spot.

sketch

pray

THIS MORNING I PRAY...

Father God,
Watch my intentions closely.
In my relationships,
Watch every step.
How easy it is for me to stray from where I started.
Give me discernment
So that I can remain consistent in
my service to others.
Amen

THIS DAY I PRAY...

Father God,
Take this humble heart
And mold it as you wish.
Make me a better servant, Father.
This is my prayer.
Don't worry about giving me what I want.
Just make me worthy to serve.

AMEN

THIS NIGHT I PRAY...

Father God,
I give you all my time.
Deliver me from worthless pursuits.
Help me see your face in those I serve.
Help me demonstrate your unfailing love
To those who stand up against me.
Give me a servant's heart.
Amen

act

A Servant's Heart. Gather together with your creative community today. Plan a day when you will serve your community by caring for those you see every day. You may want to volunteer to serve a meal in the cafeteria on your campus, allowing those who work in the cafeteria to be served by you. You may want to volunteer to clean up the gym or the bleachers after a game. Be creative and use your sketch space to document your brainstorming.

Commit to doing two things that seem small. Commit to carrying a reusable, stainless-steel water bottle instead of ever buying plastic. Commit to using cloth napkins instead of paper.

sketch

pray

THIS MORNING I PRAY…

"Long enough, God—
you've ignored me long enough.
I've looked at the back of your head long enough.
Long enough I've carried this ton of trouble,
lived with a stomach full of pain.
Long enough my arrogant enemies have
looked down their noses at me.
Take a good look at me, God, my God;
I want to look life in the eye,
So no enemy can get the best of me or
laugh when I fall on my face.
I've thrown myself headlong into your arms—
I'm celebrating your rescue.
I'm singing at the top of my lungs,
I'm so full of answered prayers."
(Psalm 13, The Message)

THIS DAY I PRAY…

Father God,
I pray that you would come.
Come, Lord Jesus, come.
Come, Lord Jesus, come.
Amen

THIS NIGHT I PRAY…

Prayer from page 6

act

The Voice of Doubt. Include in your sketch space a list of your problems with God. Don't be afraid to write out your every frustration, whether it is unanswered prayer or all-out silence from him. Be honest with yourself and be specific in creating your list. Make an appointment with a friend or a mentor to talk about your list candidly.

There are certain indoor plants that can remove toxins from the air you and your family breathe. Do some research, and then plant and maintain one or two of these plants in your home.

sketch

PLEASE GO TO PAGE 6 FOR MORNING PRAYER

sketch

pray

THIS MORNING I PRAY…
Father God,
I pray that as I still my soul
And am silent,
I might hear you.
Amen

THIS DAY I PRAY…
Listen to the cries of the created
    world and be silent.

THIS NIGHT I PRAY…
Listen to the cries of God's children
    who are in need of rescue and be silent.

act

Active Listening. This week you will engage in a prayer life of active listening. This means being silent and allowing God to settle around you. Your sketch space will be important this week because you will want to document the things God shows you as you are led into silent prayer with words and images. Please keep your routine of morning, daily, and nightly prayer. Also, join with your creative community and engage in the actions that you or they feel led to do through your prayer time.

sketch

There's a day coming
when the mountain of God's House
Will be The Mountain—
solid, towering over all mountains.
All nations will river toward it,
people from all over set out for it.
They'll say, "Come,
let's climb God's Mountain,
go to the House of the God of Jacob.
He'll show us the way he works
so we can live the way we're made."

—ISAIAH 2:1-5 (THE MESSAGE)

Out of the depths I cry to you, O Lord;

O Lord, hear my voice.

Let your ears be attentive

to my cry for mercy.

If you, O Lord, kept a record of sins,

O Lord, who could stand?

But with you there is forgiveness;

therefore you are feared.

I wait for the Lord, my soul waits,

and in his word I put my hope.

My soul waits for the Lord

more than watchmen wait for the morning,

more than watchmen wait for the morning.

O Israel, put your hope in the Lord,

for with the Lord is unfailing love

and with him is full redemption.

He himself will redeem Israel

from all their sins.

—PSALM 130 (NIV)

Read Daniel 3.

sketch

Look! I see four men walking around in the fire, unbound and unharmed, and the fourth looks like a son of the gods.

—DANIEL 3:25 (NIV)

Behold, I will create

new heavens and a new earth.

The former things will not be remembered,

nor will they come to mind.

But be glad and rejoice forever

in what I will create,

for I will create Jerusalem to be a delight

and its people a joy.

—ISAIAH 65:17-18 (NIV)

Before they call I will answer;

while they are still speaking I will hear.

The wolf and the lamb will feed together,

and the lion will eat straw like the ox,

but dust will be the serpent's food.

They will neither harm nor destroy

on all my holy mountain,"

says the Lord.

—ISAIAH 65:24-25 (NIV)

They will build houses and dwell in them;

they will plant vineyards and eat their fruit.

—ISAIAH 65:21 (NIV)

New Heaven and New Earth. What does it look like?
Draw images that come to mind when you read Isaiah 65.

PLEASE GO TO PAGE 6 FOR MORNING PRAYER

sketch

Kingdom Come.
What does it look like to you?

PLEASE GO TO PAGE 6 FOR MORNING PRAYER

sketch

The Word became flesh and blood,
and moved into the neighborhood.
We saw the glory with our own eyes,
the one-of-a-kind glory,
like Father, like Son,
Generous inside and out,
true from start to finish.

—JOHN 1:14 (THE MESSAGE)

presence

pray

THIS MORNING I PRAY…

Lord Jesus,
Your mercy flows over me like waves.
You have looked at me in all my filth
And decided to be near anyway.
It is just how you said,
Just how you promised.
God's presence.
Amen

THIS DAY I PRAY…

Lord Jesus,
I give you my time,
That I might live out my moments
In intentional worship.
Amen

THIS NIGHT I PRAY…

Father God,
You have made your light to shine upon us.
You have made a way for our paths to be straight.
You have sent us the Rabbi.
Help me to listen closely
And to follow closely.
So that people might see me
And know him.
Amen

act

Christmas Celebration. Join together with your creative community and plan a Christmas celebration. It doesn't matter what time of year it is. Go all out, with trees and lights. Invite your friends and family to come. Make sure to include these things at your gathering:

- A reading of the birth of Christ from the book of Luke.

- Songs of worship sung together celebrating Jesus' coming.

 Make sure that your Christmas party is a green one by using energy-saving LED lights, getting a pesticide-free tree, and eating organic and local foods.

sketch

pray

THIS MORNING I PRAY...
Lord Jesus,
Prepare me.
Amen

THIS DAY I PRAY...
Lord Jesus,
I give you my time,
That I might spend it
In preparation of your coming.

THIS NIGHT I PRAY...
Father God,
Allow your Spirit to rest upon me.
Prepare me,
So that I might bring good news to the broken
And ease the burdens of those who are weighed down.
Prepare me for action.
Amen

act

Our Temptation. The moment Jesus is baptized, he heads out into the wild to be tempted. Satan doesn't tempt Jesus with things he wouldn't be interested in. He tempts him with things that Jesus would find it hard to say no to. Is it the same for you? Use your sketch space to depict some of your greatest temptations. As Jesus did in the wild, begin a 40-day fast from something today. This is to prepare you as we begin to dig deeper into the life of Christ.

Look around your room. As you do, use your remaining sketch space to list some things you bought on impulse and never use, wear, or dust. Write out a commitment to yourself to avoid impulse buying and only purchase what you need.

sketch

pray

THIS MORNING I PRAY…
Lord Jesus,
Teach me to pray like you.
Help me to quiet myself as much as I can manage
And seek you in the stillness,
In the midst of all the craziness.
Be my quiet place.
Amen

THIS DAY I PRAY…
Lord Jesus,
I give you my time,
That I might spend it in constant prayer.
Amen

THIS NIGHT I PRAY…
Father God,
In the stillness I meet with you,
And I pray as you instructed.
Amen

act

Place of Prayer. Jesus was always surrounded by crowds yet always found the time to withdraw to secluded places and pray. If you haven't done this already, spend your morning, day, or night prayer in a place where you know no one will bother you. Include in your sketch space some reasons why you enjoy this type of prayer.

 **Natural light is a wonderful resource.** It's free and abundant. Break your habit of turning on the lights every time you enter a room. Use your remaining sketch space to write out some thoughts and feelings you have about relying on the sun as your main source of light.

sketch

pray

THIS MORNING I PRAY...

Lord Jesus,
Guide my steps—every single one.
Give me wisdom in my relationships.
And give me good friends—
People who hold me up
As I, in turn, hold them up.
Amen

THIS DAY I PRAY...

Lord Jesus,
I give you my time,
That I might spend it enjoying great friends.
Amen

THIS NIGHT I PRAY...

Father God,
Help me to befriend the friendless,
    as you did,
Instead of jockeying for popularity,
    as you never did.
Help my friends to see a reflection of your life in me
And for me to see the same in them.
I pray that we might teach each other how to love.
Amen

act

Life As A Boat. Use your sketch space to draw a boat. Then think of your life as this boat. Who would be the crew members aboard this vessel? How do they help the boat stay above water? Jesus was intentional with taking time to choose and cultivate friendships. Thinking about your crew members, jot down some ways that these people bring the best out of you and some ways that you can better generate the best out of them. Pray that God will help you reevaluate your relationships with this mentality.

 **Rainwater is another abundant resource.** Research some creative ways to collect and reuse the rain that falls on your rooftop and the rooftop of your school.

sketch

Heal the sick, raise the dead, cleanse those who have leprosy, drive out demons. Freely you have received, freely give.

—MATTHEW 10:8

pray

THIS MORNING I PRAY...

Lord Jesus,
Though we were severely contagious,
You touched us and carried our disease.
I pray that I might embody that kind of love.
Amen

THIS DAY I PRAY...

Lord Jesus,
I give you my time,
That I might spend it healing the wounded.
Amen

THIS NIGHT I PRAY...

Father God,
Forgive me for spending all my time with the healthy
While ignoring the sick.
What good is that anyway?
It's like a bandage on a wound that's been
        healed long ago.
It's useless.
Use me to help stop the bleeding in this world.
Amen

act

A Healing Touch. Join together with your creative community and plan a trip to the hospital to visit those who are terminally ill. Decide on some entertainment you can provide for them and some gifts you can bring. An idea would be to act as if it is Christmas, wearing hats and singing carols. Be creative but not disrespectful. Remember, the important thing is that, with your presence, you are bringing healing to people who might be struggling to find hope. Include in your sketch space some relationships that were born from this experience and some things you are doing each day to bring healing in your community and environment.

Check your house's windows and doors for drafts. Drafts cause your house to expend a much greater amount of energy in heating and cooling. Research ways to seal drafts, even if you have to get creative. Your parents won't care. You're saving them money!

sketch

pray

THIS MORNING I PRAY...
Lord Jesus,
You have not healed me so that I can
    hide myself away.
You have not chosen me to sit on the sidelines.
You have called me to move,
To hear and tell stories.
I ask only that I might remain in your presence
    as I roam.
Amen

THIS DAY I PRAY...
Lord Jesus,
I give you my time.
Amen

THIS NIGHT I PRAY...
Prayer from page 6

act

Roaming in Tandem. Within your creative community, pair off with a partner of the same sex. Plan a trip together. It may be a trip to visit a national landmark or visit a relative nearby. It may be for a weekend or maybe just a day. After Jesus had spent some time in ministry with his disciples, he sent them out in twos to practice the things they had learned. Do the same. As you journey, discuss your experience and what God is showing you as you think and pray on things like worship, prayer, relationships, and healing. Afterwards, join together and share your stories.

Find someone to carpool with as much as you can. Maybe you go to school with someone who lives close to you. How much sense does it make for you both to drive? This will not only reduce fuel emissions but could spark a new friendship.

sketch

PLEASE GO TO PAGE 6 FOR MORNING PRAYER

sketch

pray

THIS MORNING I PRAY...
Lord Jesus,
Give me the courage to live this out.
Amen

THIS DAY I PRAY...
Lord Jesus,
Give me the courage to live this out.
Amen.

THIS NIGHT I PRAY...
Lord Jesus,
Give me the courage to live this out.
Amen

act

Words to Build a Life On. One day Jesus walked up on a mountainside, sat down, and delivered the greatest sermon in history. Read Matthew 5-7 with your creative community, or by yourself in an out-of-the-way place. Make a commitment today to memorize this entire section of the Bible. It may seem impossible, but it's not, and it's worth it.

Look around your house, in drawers, in your garage, even in your trashcan. Use your sketch space to come up with some ideas for reusing the items you see that will eventually go to waste.

sketch

Let me tell you why you are here. You're here to be salt-seasoning that brings out the God-flavors of this earth.

—MATTHEW 5:13 (THE MESSAGE)

pray

THIS MORNING I PRAY…

Lord Jesus,
Help me to live blessed.
I pray that my "cleansed and grateful life"
Would point people to you.
Amen

THIS DAY I PRAY…

Lord Jesus,
You did not come so I could hide the colors
    you revealed.
You came so that I might shine brightly
    before people.
This might feel awkward and vulnerable,
But you have called me to be open.
You have called me to be salt and light.
So I will do it.
Amen

THIS NIGHT I PRAY…

(Read Matthew 5-7)
Lord Jesus,
Give us the strength to live this out.
Amen

act

Open House. Gather together with your creative community. Plan an open house/art show where each member will be displaying a painting, drawing, short story, poem, song, dance, whatever to share the change that has taken place in their lives because of God's presence. Hold this event anywhere you are able—maybe at your church, on your campus, or in a local venue of some kind.

 Have a reusable-tote-bag-making competition. Host it at your school or in your community. The rules will be simple—a prize to the person who uses reusable materials to make the coolest, most creative tote.

sketch

pray

THIS MORNING I PRAY...

Lord Jesus,
Help me never to be satisfied with
    a decent relationship with you.
I pray that I might always be looking for
    ways to go beyond…
Beyond what is expected,
Beyond what is churchy,
Beyond what is sufficient,
to what is radically Jesus-like.
Amen

THIS DAY I PRAY...

Lord Jesus,
Humble me.
Guard me from the need to be right.
Protect me from the need to be accepted.
Rescue me from the need to be cool.
Help me to be perfect, as you are perfect.
Amen

THIS NIGHT I PRAY…

(Read Matthew 5-7)
Lord Jesus,
Give us the strength to live this out.
Amen

act

Perfectly Strange. It's easy and comfortable for us to hang out with the people we enjoy. It doesn't require much effort. Placing ourselves in the midst of people we don't necessarily enjoy or people who have hurt us is substantially more difficult. Use your sketch space to jot down some names that come to mind when you think about this. Seek out those people, and ask if there is a time you can have a conversation about what you can do to mend the broken relationship. This will not be comfortable, and people will find it strange, but Jesus' petition is that we be decidedly different from the norm.

 Talk with your family about making it a policy to have the lights out during the day and the thermostat turned down in the evening. This will save money and energy, and you will be surprised how well your comfort level adapts.

sketch

pray

THIS MORNING I PRAY...
Lord Jesus,
Steer me clear of "that kind" of faith;
The kind that is on display;
The kind that looks so polished and clean
but is actually rotting within.
Help me never to worry about
    being a crowd pleaser
But instead to honestly and simply seek you.
Amen

THIS DAY I PRAY...
Lord Jesus,
Penetrate beneath the surface in my life.
I pray that you would genuinely know me.
Forgive me for all the posing I have done.
I don't want that anymore.
I no longer wish to "act" out my faith
    as if on a stage.
Take me away from the crowd.
Amen

THIS NIGHT I PRAY...
(Read Matthew 5-7)
Lord Jesus,
Give us the strength to live this out.
Amen

act

Secret Giving. Include in your sketch space some things God is showing you through your fasting. Also include some things God has shown you through your times of secluded prayer. This week, give an anonymous gift or donation to a friend or charity. Use your sketch space to jot down some thoughts and emotions that come from doing this.

If you are paying monthly bills, switch them all to paperless/online billing so the paper, energy, and fuel used to send you the bill can be spared.

sketch

pray

THIS MORNING I PRAY...

Lord Jesus,
Help me to relax,
Free from worrying about
Looking cool,
Acting cool,
Having this,
Having that.
Capture my full attention, Jesus.
Amen

THIS DAY I PRAY...

Lord Jesus,
Forgive me for misplacing my treasure.
Break me of these habits
So that I can worship you
And only you.
Amen

THIS NIGHT I PRAY...

(Read Matthew 5-7)
Lord Jesus,
Give us the strength to live this out.
Amen

act

 Fashion Fast. Include in your sketch space some thoughts that come to mind when you consider the word *treasure*. Keep in mind the culture in which you live. Can you think of some instances where materialism has caused pain in this world?

Go vintage. Shop at thrift stores. This helps to support local economy and perpetuates the reuse of otherwise discarded items.

sketch

pray

THIS MORNING I PRAY…

Lord Jesus,
Help me to build my life around these words.
Plant me deeply in them, I pray,
So that I am not led astray by fakers;
So that I am not tossed around by tough times;
So that I can be a wise and genuine follower,
Rather than a mask-wearing hypocrite.
Amen

THIS DAY I PRAY…

Lord Jesus,
Give us the strength to live this out.
Amen

THIS NIGHT I PRAY…

Prayer from page 6

act

Living in Contrast. Make some time to meet with a friend and go over Matthew 5-7. Maybe even practice reciting back and forth what you have been able to memorize. Together list some things that Jesus taught that are different from what you see in your lives and the lives of those around you. Hint: your list might be very long. What does this tell you about the way Jesus calls us to live? Together, pray about this.

Spend some time among nature today. Maybe even draw a bit in your sketch space, as you are inspired or troubled by what you see. How has your attitude changed as you have become more in tune with the wounds in the environment?

sketch

PLEASE GO TO PAGE 6 FOR MORNING PRAYER

sketch

pray

THIS MORNING I PRAY...

Lord Jesus,
I pray that my faith might be great,
Instead of fickle and fleeting.
Examine the intent behind my doubts
    and questions,
And help me to open my eyes to
    the proof that is all around.
Amen

THIS DAY I PRAY...

Lord Jesus,
Open my eyes to the miracles in my life.
Forgive me for missing or overlooking them.
Amen

THIS NIGHT I PRAY...

Father God,
Find in me a faithful servant,
No matter the circumstances.
Within your presence, there is healing beyond what
    I can imagine,
And that is where I want to be.
I believe.
Help me with my unbelief.
Amen

act

Open Eyes. Jesus often rebukes the disciples for having little faith because they require miraculous signs to believe Jesus is who he says he is. Can you relate? Use your sketch space to jot down some things that cause you to doubt. Afterwards, think about all the things that you can count on happening every day—things like the sun rising, the friends or family members who love you, or the basic needs that have been supplied for you. Could it be that God is performing miracles all around that you are overlooking?

Roll down the windows in your car and cut the AC. Put your hand out the window and let the wind run through your fingers. Enjoy.

sketch

pray

THIS MORNING I PRAY…

Lord Jesus,
I pray that I might recognize your touch
  in this world
As a touch that changes things,
Makes clean what was once contaminated.
Forgive me for explaining it away
  or calling it other things.
Help me to have faith like a child.
So that I might never cease being amazed by you.
Amen

THIS DAY I PRAY…

Lord Jesus,
Help me to believe that with one touch I am healed.
Amen

THIS NIGHT I PRAY…

Lord Jesus,
Give me the courage to reach for your cloak.
It might mean that I will be exposed,
Brought out from my comfortable hiding place.
It might mean that I will be vulnerable,
But I have been secretly bleeding for far too long.
I pray for one touch and believe that it's enough.
Amen

act

It's hard to turn on the news for two seconds and not be filled with grief. There is so much bad news in the world that our media seems to feast upon. But every once in a while, a miracle story manages to shine through. Gather clippings from the Internet or newspaper (in black and white) that document some of these stories, and then gather with your creative community and create a huge wall of these clippings, using tape and a piece of cardboard or an actual wall. Then use crayons, colored pencils, or markers to color the wall together like you might have when you were kids.

Instead of throwing away old newspapers, save them. Newspaper is a creative and cost-efficient way to wrap presents.

sketch

Use your sketch space to journal about some place in your life where you need healing. Do you believe that one touch from Jesus is enough? Read: Matthew 9:18-23

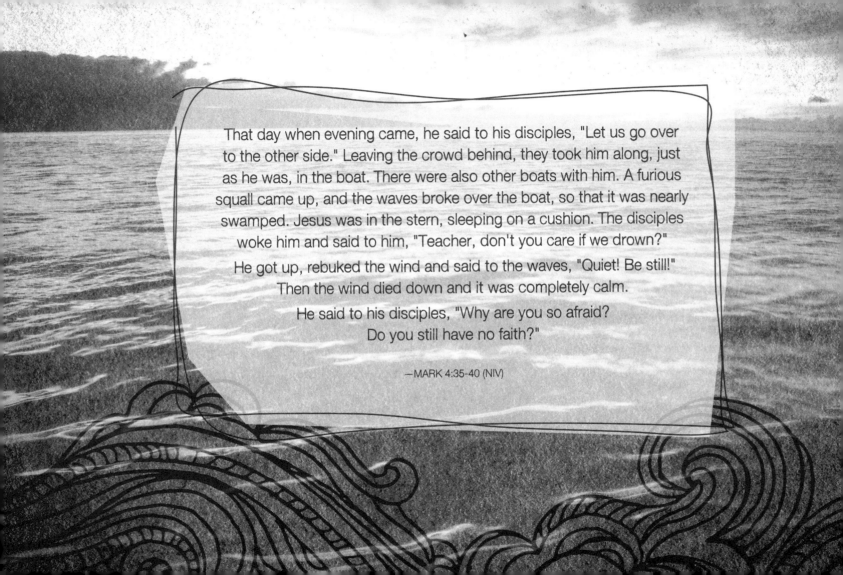

That day when evening came, he said to his disciples, "Let us go over to the other side." Leaving the crowd behind, they took him along, just as he was, in the boat. There were also other boats with him. A furious squall came up, and the waves broke over the boat, so that it was nearly swamped. Jesus was in the stern, sleeping on a cushion. The disciples woke him and said to him, "Teacher, don't you care if we drown?"

He got up, rebuked the wind and said to the waves, "Quiet! Be still!" Then the wind died down and it was completely calm.

He said to his disciples, "Why are you so afraid? Do you still have no faith?"

—MARK 4:35-40 (NIV)

pray

THIS MORNING I PRAY…
Lord Jesus,
However the wind may blow, you are still love.
Amen

THIS DAY I PRAY…
(Read and think about this in silence)

> Then they cried out to the Lord in their trouble,
> and he brought them out of their distress.
> He stilled the storm to a whisper;
> the waves of the sea were hushed.
> They were glad when it grew calm,
> and he guided them to their desired haven.
> —Psalm 107:28-30 (NIV)

THIS NIGHT I PRAY…

> God, my shepherd! I don't need a thing.
> You have bedded me down in lush meadows,
> you find me quiet pools to drink from.
> True to your word, you let me catch my breath
> and send me in the right direction.
> Even when the way goes through
> Death Valley, I'm not afraid when you walk at my side.
> Your trusty shepherd's crook makes me feel secure.
> You serve me a six-course dinner
> right in front of my enemies.
> You revive my drooping head;
> my cup brims with blessing.
> Your beauty and love chase after me
> every day of my life.
> I'm back home in the house of God for
> the rest of my life.
> —Psalm 23 (The Message)

act

In the Boat. Imagine you were one of the disciples in the boat the day Jesus calmed the storm. What would you be thinking and feeling? Write a short story from this perspective—as if you were in the boat. Meet with a friend and share your stories. Include in your sketch space some storms taking place in your life, the life of your community, or around the world where it is hard to picture God at work. What is Jesus' reaction to this kind of doubt?

The next storm that hits, turn off all the lights and anything in your house that creates noise. Then sit, watch, and listen.

sketch

pray

THIS MORNING I PRAY...

Lord Jesus,
Help me be a voice of truth.
Help me have a healing touch.
Help me do your work
And believe that you are in me,
Working through me.
Amen

THIS DAY I PRAY...

Lord Jesus,
I can do all things through you.
Tame my fears and anxieties.
Overwhelm them with your spirit,
Which fills me with love for others.
Help my acts to be evidence of that love—
That one great love.
Amen

THIS NIGHT I PRAY...

Holy Spirit,
Fill me to the brim
And then even more,
So that truth and life would spill out of me
And on to those around me.
Amen

act

Present in the Impossible. Jesus lived a lifestyle of making the impossible possible—making the blind see, making the wicked change their ways. For the most part, he did this by taking time to be present in the lives of individuals who were in need of rescue. This was his life's work, and it is to be ours as well. Include in your sketch space three impossible names—people you know who are in the midst of impossible circumstances. Taking your cues from what you have learned of Jesus' life and work, how can you bring about change by being present with them?

Don't throw away your old bread. Break it up into crumbs and take it outside for the birds.

sketch

pray

THIS MORNING I PRAY…

Lord Jesus,
Make me a fisher of souls.
Help to have the kind of faith
That leads people to ask questions.
Give me the ability to answer
In wisdom, gentleness, and love.
I pray that, like you, people may find in me
Something different.
Amen

THIS DAY I PRAY…

Lord Jesus,
Surely, they will push against me.
I will lean on you.
Surely, they will throw stones.
I will trust in you.
Surely, they will outwit me.
I will rely on you.
Surely, they will find me flawed.
I will rest on you.
Amen

THIS NIGHT I PRAY…

Lord Jesus,
Make me a fisher of souls,
A seeker of the lost,
In wisdom, gentleness, and love.
Amen

act

Taking Questions. Gather together with your creative community. Organize a night where you will act as a panel, openly taking questions about your faith. You might be able to do this somewhere on your campus. If not, try to arrange using a public space somewhere in your community. Places like coffee shops, recreation centers, or theaters would be great. Make it a place where people will feel comfortable coming, and publicize it widely on your campus and in your community.

I know this is a terrifying task, so pray together for these three things.

- That God would help you be open with your lives and stories.

- That the Spirit would fill you completely so that your words would be his.

- That people would come who are in great need of hearing good news.

Plan a day of environmental service that your creative community can orchestrate in your community. Whether it is planting trees, planting gardens, or making repairs to local businesses to increase energy efficiency, the important thing is your group's presence among the community, making things better.

sketch

pray

THIS MORNING I PRAY…
Lord Jesus,
I want to love you with all my life.
It's weird to say, and it's hard to do.
I know it will cost me the life I want.
I know it may cause me pain.
I know it may lead me places I don't want to go.
I choose to follow.
Amen

THIS DAY I PRAY…
Lord Jesus,
Give me the courage to live this out.
Agape.
Amen

THIS NIGHT I PRAY…
Prayer from page 6

act

Use your sketch space to write the word *AGAPE* in whatever manner you wish. This is a Greek word for love—but not just any kind of love. This is the kind of love that comes with no strings attached. It is much more than a physical love or a brotherly love. *Agape* is the kind of love that takes everything we have and asks for nothing in return. This is the kind of love Jesus displayed. Use your sketch space to jot down some thoughts and images that come to mind when you consider *agape*. What scares you about it?

Use your sketch space to describe some things you love about nature. Ask some friends what their favorite things are about nature and listen to their responses.

sketch

PLEASE GO TO PAGE 6 FOR MORNING PRAYER

sketch

pray

THIS MORNING I PRAY…

Lord Jesus,
Help me to walk like you
And live a life of sacrifice.
This is not about me.
There is a much bigger picture here,
That I am just a piece of.
Amen

THIS DAY I PRAY…

Lord Jesus,
Give me a spirit that cries out:
As long as people are being healed,
As long as people are coming to you,
As long as restoration is happening,
Then it is well with my soul.
Amen

THIS NIGHT I PRAY…

Lord Jesus,
You are good all the time.
Amen

act

Read the story of John the Baptist—Matthew 3:1-17. Use your sketch space to track your thoughts about this character.

One Page. Go with a friend or group of friends to a bookstore or library. Being as quiet as possible (in regards to those around you), go to the fiction section, picking out books at random. When you have collected a few, sit together and read one single page from the books you chose. Then attempt to tell your friend(s) what those books are about from the single page that you read.

This is a fun exercise, but the point is very important. A large part of living a life of sacrifice is grasping the idea that your life is a small yet necessary part of a very large story. Use your sketch space to jot down some connections you see between the exercise and this idea.

Before you buy a new book, always check to see if there is a used copy available online or in a used bookstore.

sketch

pray

THIS MORNING I PRAY…

Lord Jesus,
You carried our sin in the form of a cross.
It was not your burden, yet you chose it.
You embraced suffering for our sake—
Denied yourself to bring rest to the weary.
Give me the courage to live like that.
Amen

THIS DAY I PRAY…

Lord Jesus,
Turn me away from self-preservation.
I pray that, in a world so full of self-seeking,
I would be different,
Ready to suffer if need be,
Ready to go without
For the sake of those in need of rescue.
Amen

THIS NIGHT I PRAY…

Lord Jesus,
You are good all the time.
Amen

act

Defining Your Cross. Use your sketch space to draw a cross. Then fill in the cross with words that define the cross Jesus carried and was nailed to for us.

Read Matthew 16:24-26. How would you define *your* cross? Use your sketch space to draw another cross, and fill it with words that define the relational, environmental, or global burdens that you take up every day. What actions are you taking to support this?

sketch

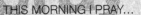

pray

THIS MORNING I PRAY…
Lord Jesus,
O, how the years have taught me
To pose and puff myself up,
To act as if I am so (fill in the blank).
I know how to play the game well.
Pull me away from my posing, Lord,
So I might be like a child again.
Amen

THIS DAY I PRAY…
Lord Jesus,
Teach me how to come to you as a child—
Openly and honestly,
Unable to hold back my excitement at
    your coming kingdom.
Amen

THIS NIGHT I PRAY…
Lord Jesus,
You are good all the time.
Amen

act

Three Stupid Questions. Use your sketch space to write out three questions you have always wondered about but have been too embarrassed to ask anyone. You know what I'm talking about—those questions you think everyone knows the answers to but you. Have one be about your faith, another about the world, and another about culture. Then gather with your creative community and go around taking turns asking your questions with complete honesty.

After the laughter dies down, think about this: *Jesus hated inauthenticity. He longed for us, like children, to always be able to ask honest questions and be honestly amazed.*

Watch out for "green washing." This is when products or businesses make generic claims about environmental friendliness that either mean nothing or cover up bigger problems. A little research should assure you that the green companies and products you support are legit.

pray

THIS MORNING I PRAY...

Lord Jesus,
Give me a humble heart.
Help me be a servant to all.
This world may offer me power,
But the prize you offer is much greater.
Help me remember that.
Amen

THIS DAY I PRAY...

Lord Jesus,
Find in me a good and faithful servant.
If I can just be faithful with a few things,
Then you will trust me with many.
Make me a good and faithful servant
So that I can share in your happiness.
Amen

THIS NIGHT I PRAY...

Lord Jesus,
You are good all the time.
Amen.

act

Shadow of a Servant. Think of a person in your community who has a thankless job—someone you would consider a humble servant. You may need to ask a friend, parent, or mentor about this if you can't think of anyone. Once you have come up with a person who fits the bill, ask them if you can shadow them for a day—doing what they do or helping them do what they do. Use your sketch space to document the activities of your day and the thoughts and emotions you felt performing this task.

Find an environmental mentor—someone who exemplifies a green lifestyle. Ask if you can meet with them often and discuss the patterns of life they have picked up over the year. Chances are, they have quite a bit of wisdom to share and would love to share it.

sketch

pray

THIS MORNING I PRAY...

Lord Jesus,

Show me the "one thing."

The thing that keeps me from following fully.

Maybe it's obvious. Maybe not.

But I pray right now it would be known.

I pray that like a guilt-riddled thief,

I would remove it from my hiding place

And lay it at your feet.

Amen

THIS DAY I PRAY...

Lord Jesus,

"One thing I ask of the Lord,

this is what I seek:

that I may dwell in the house of the Lord

all the days of my life,

to gaze upon the beauty of the Lord

and to seek him in his temple."

—Psalm 27:4

Amen

THIS NIGHT I PRAY...

Lord Jesus,

You are good all the time.

Amen

act

One Thing. Read the story of the rich young ruler (Mark 10:17-29). Use your sketch space to jot down some ways you can relate to the young man in the story. What is the "one thing" in your life? Maybe it's more than one.

Think and pray about this. This is very important. Before Jesus explains the "one thing" the young ruler lacks, the verse says, "Jesus looked at him and loved him."

 Limit your household to one trash bag this week. This will force you to think about every single thing you throw away. Could it be reused, recycled, decomposed? Could you do this for longer than a week?

pray

THIS MORNING I PRAY…

Lord Jesus,
Through the cross you made it possible.
With pierced hands, feet, and side,
You made it so that I might walk through a field of dirt
And come out with clean feet.
I can't understand it, but I accept it
Because I long to be a part of what you're doing.
Thank you.
Amen

THIS DAY I PRAY…

This is my prayer forever and always.
> "May I never boast except in the cross of our Lord
> Jesus Christ, through which the world has been
> crucified to me, and I to the world."
> —Galatians 6:14

THIS NIGHT I PRAY…

Prayer from page 6

act

The Ministry of Foot Washing. Join together with your creative community and plan a day of foot washing on your campus or in your city. This is exactly as it sounds. Partner up with a friend or mentor and decide on a day when you will go out and have a foot-washing booth. This can be done very simply with a bowl of water, a jug of water to refill the bowl after each washing, a number of clean towels, and a sign.

If you are asked why you are doing this, reference John 13:1-12.

The items of clothing you probably wash more than anything else are your socks and underwear. Make a commitment to washing these things by hand once every other week instead of doing a load of laundry. This will save energy and water.

sketch

PLEASE GO TO PAGE 6 FOR MORNING PRAYER

sketch

satisfied

pray

THIS MORNING I PRAY…

Risen Lord,
You have made all things new—
A whole new plan for the world.
I am not condemned.
I am justified.
I am not ashamed.
I am redeemed.
I don't have to look at my scars in sorrow,
But instead I can rejoice because of your
infinite grace.
Amen

THIS DAY I PRAY…

Risen Lord,
I pray that I might accept new life as
freely as you give it.
Help me to dive in headfirst
Instead of tiptoeing around the edges.
Your rivers of grace flow around me.
I am covered completely.
And when I emerge, I am a new person.
Amen

THIS NIGHT I PRAY…

Lord Jesus,
"Therefore, if anyone is in Christ he is a new
creation; the old is gone, the new has come!"
—2 Corinthians 5:17
Amen

act

Coloring Grace. This week you will be using your sketch space to literally color grace. Today fill the G with symbols of the shame you carry that grace relieves you of. Think about this: *What would it look like to live completely justified?*

Use your remaining sketch space to draw a picture of your garden.

sketch

pray

THIS MORNING I PRAY…

Risen Lord,

You are the ultimate sacrifice.

There is no more needed.

Help me embrace what it means to live in that truth

Today and every day.

Amen

THIS DAY I PRAY…

Risen Lord,

Your sacrifice is complete.

May my life be an offering of praise.

In all that I do, help me to remember

My encounter with grace.

Amen

THIS NIGHT I PRAY…

Lord Jesus,

You are my eternal dwelling place.

Your spilled blood opened the door

So that I could come in and stay forever.

Your law is written upon my heart

As my sins slide away from your memory.

I am home.

Amen

act

Coloring Grace, Day 2. Fill the *R* with images, symbols, colors, or words that remind you of God's ultimate sacrifice. Think about this: *We can't do anything to earn grace. It was meant to be given freely.*

 Is there one thing you have been holding back on changing to make your life's rhythm more environmentally healthy because of the sacrifice you will have to make? Use your sketch space to write out some of your honest hesitancies. Writing out these worries might bring to light just how small they are in contrast to the importance of you doing your part to be a better steward. Maybe it's time.

sketch

pray

THIS MORNING I PRAY…

Risen Lord,

Help me be bold in my assurance of you.

I pray that signs of your forgiveness would fill my life,

That your spirit would radiate out of me and
transform me.

Amen

THIS DAY I PRAY…

Risen Lord,

Cover me.

Amen

THIS NIGHT I PRAY…

Lord Jesus,

Because of your amazing grace, I can be bold.

I can come with a face unveiled before you,

More confident in this than anything:

That you have saved me,

Justified me and made me new.

Made me new.

Because where the Spirit is,

There is freedom.

Cover me forever and ever.

Amen

act

Coloring Grace, Day 3. Today you color the A of grace. So pick a color that reminds you of the spirit inside of you—the spirit who is Jesus Christ. Then use your remaining sketch space to explain why you chose the color you did with words or images. Today make an effort to display that color to the world with the clothes you wear, the color of your nails, the color of your hair, whatever. Be creative and let this be a symbol to you of how the Spirit is to be displayed through you each day. You are to be covered with him.

Recycling and reusing glass is an imperative part of going green because glass takes a million years to decompose. Use your remaining sketch space to write or draw out plans for cool ways to reuse the glass in your home.

sketch

pray

THIS DAY I PRAY…

Risen Lord,
I rise and come to you in my weaknesses.
So that, in them, I am strong.
Amen

THIS DAY I PRAY…

Risen Lord,

"Therefore I will boast all the more gladly about my
weaknesses, so that Christ's power may rest on me.
That is why, for Christ's sake, I delight in weaknesses,
in insults, in hardships, in persecutions, in difficulties.
For when I am weak, then I am strong."
—–2 Corinthians 12:9-10 (NIV)

THIS NIGHT I PRAY…

Lord Jesus,
Help me empty myself
Of all the things that lead me to boast in myself
So that the firm foundation of my confidence
Would be found in you.
In my social circles,
On my sports teams,
In my groups and clubs,
In my church,
In this world,
Empty me of myself, so that people might see you
Radiating from my life.
Amen

act

Coloring Grace, Day 4. Leave the *C* in your sketch space empty. Now that you have spent
time working through the life of Jesus, go back over what you studied and fill the space
around the *C* with examples of times that Jesus displayed power in situations the world
would call weakness. You may want to join with some members of your creative community
to do this. I will get you started with a couple: *Jesus hung out with the outcasts instead of
seeking social status. Jesus touched those considered unclean. Jesus died on a cross…*
Now you go. Let your empty *C* be in recognition of how Jesus emptied himself out.

Be responsible about how your electronics get power. Buy only rechargeable batter-
ies, and make sure everything is turned completely off overnight.

sketch

pray

THIS MORNING I PRAY...

Risen Lord,
Help me to give like someone
    who has received a great gift
Because that is who I am.
Amen

THIS DAY I PRAY...

Risen Lord,
How could I experience your gift of grace
And not give thanks?
How could I experience the magnitude
    of your love
And not allow it to pour onto others?
How could I be given your full and
    unhindered blessing
And not be moved to give as you give?
Lord, find in me a cheerful giver.
Amen

THIS NIGHT I PRAY...

Lord Jesus,
Soften my heart
So that I might be generous in all occasions.
Amen

act

Coloring Grace, Day 5. Today you are coloring the *E* in your sketch space. Use words, images, or both to depict a healthy and growing garden. One essential response to grace is giving. We are to give as if we are planting a garden. If you are planting a garden and hold back on the seeds, you're likely to be disappointed. But if you sow generously, your return is likely to be great. In your remaining sketch space, share a story about your giving and what you have gotten in return.

Did you know that planting certain things side by side increases the productivity of your garden? Do some research and find out what you can do to get the most from your personal and community gardens.

sketch

pray

THIS MORNING I PRAY…

Risen Lord,
I think of the bread and remember
How your body was broken.
I think of the wine and remember
How you were completely poured out for us.
Amen

THIS DAY I PRAY…

Risen Lord,
I pray for those
Who might drink
And those who might eat.
I pray that they will believe.
Amen

THIS NIGHT I PRAY…

Prayer from page 6

act

Day of Communion. Gather together with your creative community. Organize a day when you will go out in pairs on your campus or in your city to share communion. For this activity you will need tables of some sort, chairs, a simple sign, a cup or cups, grape juice, and bread. Bring supplies to make sure things stay clean and plenty of juice and bread. Basically you will set up a stand where passersby can partake in the elements if they so choose. Take this seriously, and ask a mentor or parent to help you organize this responsibly. Use your sketch space to journal about this experience.

Make sure all the supplies you use to serve communion are recyclable or reusable.

sketch

PLEASE GO TO PAGE 6 FOR MORNING PRAYER

sketch

pray

THIS MORNING I PRAY…

Risen Lord,

Help us to place our hope in grace alone.

Help us not hold tight to the riches of this world

Or to waste our time with arrogant pursuits.

Instead, I pray that we might find complete satisfaction
and enjoyment

In the life that is real; The life that you alone can give.

Amen

THIS DAY I PRAY…

Risen Lord,

O God, you are my God,

earnestly I seek you;

my soul thirsts for you,

my body longs for you,

in a dry and weary land

where there is no water.

I have seen you in the sanctuary

and beheld your power and your glory.

Because your love is better than life,

my lips will glorify you.

I will praise you as long as I live,

and in your name I will lift up my hands.

My soul will be satisfied as with the richest of foods;

with singing lips my mouth will praise you.

—Psalm 63:1-5 (NIV)

Amen

THIS NIGHT I PRAY…

My soul will be satisfied as with the richest of foods;

with singing lips, my mouth will praise you.

Amen

act

Use the space around the C in your sketch space to brainstorm with thoughts or images how you feel the world sees the "good life." Use the space inside the C in the same way to show how Jesus' life and actions depicted the "good life." Get together with a group of friends to discuss and pray about this.

Reference these verses in your discussion: 1 Timothy 6:17-19

 Practice the art of giving stuff away today. A great way to implement the practice of reusing is to let people reuse the stuff you never use. Look around your room. List some stuff you have and never use and then next to it, place the name of a person you can give it to.

sketch

pray

THIS MORNING I PRAY…
Risen Lord,
I pray for those who are grieving.
Even now, I pray for those who weep.
My prayer is that they might find joy;
A joy that surpasses understanding;
A joy that is complete;
A joy that can be asked for and received.
I pray this for my brothers and sisters.
Amen

THIS DAY I PRAY…
Risen Lord,
I ask, in your name, that I might have joy;
True joy;
The joy of a risen and living Christ;
The joy that no one can take away.
Amen

THIS NIGHT I PRAY…
Lord Jesus,
I pray that the world might rejoice
Because of your plan to, again,
Make all things new.
Amen

act

Joyful Noise. Today make 10 loud joyful noises as you go through your day. Some sugges-tions: *Woohoo! Yeeeaaaah!* Use the inside of the *H* in your sketch space to jot down the joyous noises you made. With your remaining sketch space, journal about this experience. Then, on your own or with friends, think about why it is difficult to be joyful and the kind of joy Jesus talked about.

Do some work in the garden today and at some point close your eyes and listen. Use your sketch space to document all that you hear. How does God show himself to you in the sounds of a growing earth?

sketch

pray

THIS MORNING I PRAY...

Risen Lord,
I pray that reconciliation would take place
Between the hurting and those who have inflicted wounds;
Between the accused and the accusers.
Help us see each other with a different point of view.
Help us to see each other as new creations.
Amen

THIS DAY I PRAY...

Risen Lord,
Make me an ambassador of reconciliation.
Make me a creator of harmony.
Amen

THIS NIGHT I PRAY...

Lord Jesus,
In this world of chaos,
Help me to hear with different ears.
Give me the ability to listen closely
To the sounds of your movements.
Strip away my worldly sight
For eyes that see with clarity and joy
The world you are embracing;
The world you are enfolding into your arms
Once again.
Amen

act

Harmony. Grab some crayons, colored pencils, or markers. Fill the A in your sketch space with colors that you feel work in perfect harmony together. Listen to your favorite song as you are doing this.

To reconcile is to bring harmony where there was once tension and separation. Jesus' ministry was one of bringing harmony between God and us. Use the remaining sketch space to jot down some ideas of things you can act out this week as a ministry of reconciliation in your relationship with the earth or with your brothers and sisters.

 Do you know that you can make your own crayons with stuff you probably have sitting in your cabinets? Do some research and see if this can be a creative way for you to reuse materials that could go to waste.

sketch

151

pray

THIS MORNING I PRAY...

Risen Lord,
Breathe hope into the lives of
    my brothers and sisters.
Use me to show them the door of your
    eternal dwelling
So that they might find rest in what is eternal
Instead of dreading the confusion of today.
Amen

THIS DAY I PRAY...

Risen Lord,
No matter what, I will not lose heart
Because I know without a doubt
That you have prepared an eternal dwelling place
    for me.

AMENTHIS NIGHT I PRAY...

Lord Jesus,
I pray that this world will be rebuilt upon the ruins,
Depending not on our own strength of
    hammer and nail
But instead completely depending on
    the blood of Christ;
The blood that built us a house.
"How lovely is your dwelling place,
    O Lord Almighty!"
Amen

act

Home. Fill the *N* in your sketch space with all the words that you associate with home. Join together with your creative community and plan a day where you will serve the homeless in your community. If you live in a community without a homeless population, plan a day where you will help those who have homes that are falling apart and in need of repair. Ask a parent, mentor, or pastor to help you plan this out. During this service day take time to ask the people you are serving what home means to them. Use your remaining sketch space to jot down some of their answers.

Take a walk outside today and thank God for his beautiful creation.

sketch

pray

THIS MORNING I PRAY...

Risen Lord,
I pray for those who long for a love that endures.
I pray that they might find it in you.
Amen

THIS DAY I PRAY...

Risen Lord,
You have shown me how to love.
Help me do it well,
At all times and in all things.
Amen

THIS NIGHT I PRAY...

Lord Jesus,
Overwhelm this world with your love.
Amen

act

Love Personified. Get a red marker, crayon, or colored pencil and color the G in your sketch space red. God loved the world so much that he gave everything. In response, we must be love personified. That means allowing the blood of Christ to cover every part of our lives—from the big decisions we make some of the time to the small ones we make all the time. Use your remaining sketch space to jot down a list of small decisions you can make to love the world better. Some suggestions: Get informed about where you shop, and do your part by not buying from companies who don't support fair trade. Turn off the water while you brush your teeth. Drive less and walk or ride your bike more. You get the idea. Take it from here.

When you have to drive, slow down. If everyone drove the speed limit, it would help immensely to decrease fuel emissions (let alone be safer).

sketch

"Love is patient, love is kind. It does not envy, it does not boast, it is not proud. It is not rude, it is not self-seeking, it is not easily angered, it keeps no record of wrongs. Love does not delight in evil but rejoices with the truth. It always protects, always trusts, always hopes, always perseveres."

—1 CORINTHIANS 13:4-7

sketch

pray

THIS MORNING I PRAY…

Risen Lord,
The waking of the day is proof once again
That you have overcome.
You have risen above death.
And by sacrificing your life, submitting yourself,
You showed just how powerless death is
And how powerful you are.
Death has lost its grip,
And I rejoice.
Amen

THIS DAY I PRAY…

Risen Lord,
You have written a new song.
You have released the slave.
You have redeemed the greatest sinner.
You have spread mercy over the nations.
You have reconciled us.
You have written a new song.
And today, I dance.
Amen

THIS NIGHT I PRAY…
PRAYER FROM PAGE 6

act

Feast and Celebrate. Fill the space inside the *S* in your sketch space with words or images that you associate with the word *feast*. Get together with your creative community and plan a meal together. Invite the mentors, parents, and pastors who have helped you through this experience. A vital part of this celebration will be sharing stories about what Jesus has shown you so far in this experience.

Encourage your parents to adopt a supermarket with management that is committed to buying locally. Develop a relationship with them and share your loyalty with others. This will give the management an argument for these healthy environmental practices and will also be beneficial financially.

sketch

PLEASE GO TO PAGE 6 FOR MORNING PRAYER

sketch

THIS MORNING I PRAY...

Holy Spirit,
Fill me to the brim and then even more so
As I take time today to wonder at your movements,
So mysterious and awesome.
You are always about the business of healing,
With gentle brushstrokes and harmonious chords.
Fill me to the brim and then even more so
So that I might be about the same.
Amen

THIS DAY I PRAY-

Holy Spirit,
Rest around us.
Amen

THIS NIGHT I PRAY...

Father God,
Set us apart for the work you have called us.
Help us not to miss it.
Fill us with joy and with the Spirit.
He is a great gift.
I pray that he might rest around us.
Amen

Art Heals. Here are some options: Go to a concert, art show, or art museum. Read a book of poetry or fiction. Listen to your favorite band or musical artist. Watch your favorite movie. Go to a play. Or think of another way to engage in your favorite form of art. Then, in your sketch space, journal about this question: *Why does art affect us the way it does?* And go a bit deeper than "I enjoy the lyrics" or "I like the colors." Why do you think moving images, or mixing colors or sounds into our ear canals can bring about change within us? How can you use art this week to bring healing to a broken situation you have witnessed?

Use the space inside the *E* in your sketch space to list some words you associate with healing.

Go to your spot in nature. Use your remaining sketch space to express how this place heals you.

sketch

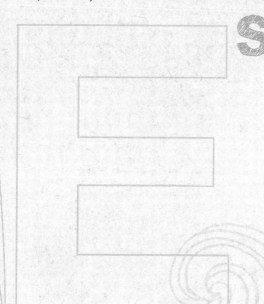

pray

THIS MORNING I PRAY…

Holy Spirit,
Fill me to the brim and then even more so.
Reside in my words
So that with them I might bring healing.
You know the situations around me.
You see the hearts that are breaking.
You share in the victories of your loved ones.
Allow that knowledge to guide my words
    for your purposes.
Amen

THIS DAY I PRAY…

Holy Spirit,
In every word we speak,
Rest around us.
In every message we send,
Rest around us.
Amen

THIS NIGHT I PRAY…

Father God,
In this world of emails and text messages,
In this world that moves so fast,
It is so easy to be careless with my words.
Help me consult the Spirit with every sound I make,
That all the messages I send
Would align with his residence inside me.
Amen

act

Words Heal. Create a postcard to give to someone today. This might be an actual postcard from some exotic place, a piece of notebook paper you draw a stick figure on, or a cool image you find online glued to a note card. Be creative. Don't worry about the image as much as the words you write on the back. Write a short message to someone you feel is in need of kind words or encouragement and give that person the postcard.

On the outside of the V in your sketch space, jot down some of the words people have said or written to you that have changed your life for the better. On the inside of the V, jot down some of the emotions you felt when those words were shared.

What do you do with old greeting cards? Make a habit of saving these and using them creatively to make your own cards.

sketch

THIS MORNING I PRAY…

Holy Spirit,
Fill me to the brim and then even more so.
Reside in every touch and every action
So that they might be nothing more
Than the outpouring of you upon those around me.
Amen

THIS DAY I PRAY…

Holy Spirit,
With every touch and every action,
Rest around us.
Amen

THIS NIGHT I PRAY…

Father God,
When I cried out with unclean lips,
You kissed me.
That is uncomfortable to say, but it's true.
You kissed and healed me through and through.
I pray that you would fill my actions with that kind of love;
A kind of love that flows out from my fingers.
I pray that we might never be content with a love that only
     speaks compassion.
I pray for a ministry of touch.
Amen

Contact. Jesus often healed people by touching them. He didn't have to. He certainly could have just said the word and made it happen; in fact, sometimes he did. But other times Jesus was intentional about touching those who needed to be healed, even if they were leprous.

Fill the inside of the *E* in your sketch space with your fingerprints. There are many ways you can do this. You might be able to get hold of an inkpad, or you could just apply some ink to the paper and then press your fingers down in it. Gather together with a friend and discuss how touch was a significant part of Jesus' ministry. What does this mean for you? Use the rest of your sketch space to jot down some notes from your conversation.

Just like making your own household cleaners, it is possible to make your own body cleansers with ingredients that are most likely sitting in your cabinets. Do some research and see if this can't be an effective way for you not only to get clean but to reduce and reuse.

sketch

pray

THIS MORNING I PRAY…

Holy Spirit,
It isn't under my own power that I wake and go
    forward.
It is with the authority that you gave me.
So I speak with confidence about the truth that I
    know,
And I pray that people might be drawn to you.
Amen

THIS DAY I PRAY…

Holy Spirit,
With the authority that we have been given,
Rest around us.
Help us to be about the business of making
    disciples.
Rest around us.
Amen

THIS NIGHT I PRAY…

Father God,
My prayer is that I might learn to share my story
With honesty and openness.
Make me a self-portrait of your unending mercy.
Allow people to see the very colors of my soul,
Into the places you have touched and healed.
The fact is this:
This story is simply too good to keep to myself.
You have satisfied the grips of death
Forever and ever.
How could I not talk about it?
Amen

act

Evangelize. It's a dirty word, isn't it? Use the area around the *R* in your sketch space to write down some thoughts and emotions you have in response to the word *evangelism*. Why do you think this is? Maybe evangelism was meant to be more of a Spirit-filled, natural thing than the forced and fake thing it has become today.

Fill the area inside the *R* in your sketch space with names of people you know are unbelievers. Pray that God would give you an opportunity to honestly and openly share your story with them. Pray that the news of Jesus' sacrifice and love would overwhelm them. Pray the Spirit would move in their lives.

Join together with your creative community and use recycled materials to create artistic posters that highlight environmental issues at your school or in your community. Ask school or city officials if it is okay for you and your friends to display your work. A good place might be a local coffee shop or other privately owned business. Use your remaining sketch space to draw some ideas.

sketch

pray

THIS MORNING I PRAY…

Holy Spirit,
Though they may throw stones,
I will not be moved.
I will sing hallelujah into the heavens.
They may laugh at me
Or cast me out.
I will sing hallelujah all the more.
I will sing hallelujah.
Amen

THIS DAY I PRAY…

Holy Spirit,
With all the negativity that comes our way,
Rest around us.
Though they may go to great lengths to stir up the waves,
I know one who quiets the waves with a few words.
"Quiet. Be still."
Amen

THIS NIGHT I PRAY…

Father God,
Forgive those who speak against me.
Soften their hearts
And also mine so that no anger would remain;
Only love.
Help me to look on those who hate me as you do.
But when it becomes too much to handle,
Be my hiding place.
Amen

act

Safe Place. Gather together with your entire creative community or just a few who are able. Have an honest and open conversation about some of the persecution you have faced because of your faith or in response to your attempts to share your story. Pray together for two things. First, thank God for the struggle. Second, pray that you might find a safe place resting in the Spirit.

Fill the area around the Y in your sketch space with images, colors, or words that you associate with a storm. Leave the inside of the Y blank. Do this as a reminder that, though they may sling stones, there is a deeper place they can't touch.

The next time you are in a coffee shop, remember this: coffee grounds make great soil. So don't just throw them out. Use them to go out and get your hands dirty in the garden.

sketch

pray

THIS MORNING I PRAY…

Holy Spirit,

"This is love: not that we loved God, but that he loved us and sent his Son as an atoning sacrifice for our sins. Dear friends, since God so loved us, we also ought to love one another. No one has ever seen God; but if we love one another, God lives in us and his love is made complete in us."
—1 John 4:10-12 (NIV)

Amen

THIS DAY I PRAY…

"There is no fear in love. But perfect love drives out fear, because fear has to do with punishment. The one who fears is not made perfect in love."
—1 John 4:18 (NIV)

Amen

THIS NIGHT I PRAY…

Prayer from page 6

act

Love Made Perfect. Encountering and embracing the Spirit means loving fearlessly. There is likely at least one thing that scares you about acting on God's mission (probably more than one). These are things you have steered clear of this whole experience. Use your sketch space to list these things. It might be the fear of being hurt, the fear of being broke (financially), the fear of being open with people, the fear of encountering those who are different from you. Center yourself around the greatest fear and then tackle it this week. Ask a friend to join you in coming up with a way to let your love rise above this fear. Use your remaining sketch space to journal on what took place.

Don't get it twisted. We are supposed to fear God in a very real way. The cool thing is that it is his love that then quells our fear of him and allows us to see him and not be destroyed. There is evidence of this all over creation. Have you ever looked up and been overwhelmed by the bigness of the sky? Use your sketch space to draw some things about nature that honestly scare you.

PLEASE GO TO PAGE 6 FOR MORNING PRAYER

sketch

pray

THIS MORNING I PRAY...

Holy Spirit,
Give me *shalom*.
Amen

THIS DAY I PRAY...

Holy Spirit,
Instill these in me:
Joy;
Gentleness;
Compassion;
Justice;
Love.
Amen

THIS NIGHT I PRAY...

Father God,
The barrier is gone between you and I.
You have destroyed the walls of chaos and revolt
And paved a path for me to walk freely.
What need is there to fret and toil?
What need is there to toss and turn
When I can rest in *shalom*?
Amen

act

The word *shalom* means peace. Use the area outside the *T* in your sketch space to jot down some thoughts and emotions you relate with the word peace. Inside the *T* is *shalom* in Hebrew. Write this on a slip of paper and carry it with you today. Take it out often and pray about what it might mean to live out *shalom*.

You see, *shalom* isn't just a state of things—like saying there is peace in the land. *Shalom* is an active way of being. *Shalom* means living in an active pursuit of wholeness and practicing things like gentleness and joy on a daily basis.

Give your car a rest. While sitting in traffic or at a stoplight for a long time, turn your car off instead of letting it idle.

sketch

שָׁלוֹם

pray

THIS MORNING I PRAY…

Holy Spirit,
Give me *shalom*.
Amen

THIS DAY I PRAY…

Holy Spirit,
Give me contentment with my place.
Lead me away from envy.
Draw me away from making comparisons.
You have instilled a unique gift inside me.
Cultivate your work within.
Trim off these unneeded things that choke
    and stunt my growth.
Help me rejoice in the gifts of my
    brothers and sisters.
Make us one body moving together.
Amen

THIS NIGHT I PRAY…

Father God,
You are so constant and steady.
Like the flowing of a river, you are peace.
I long for the steadiness.
I look around and get distracted by the wrong things.
The gifts of others make me jealous.
The abilities of others cause me to doubt you.
Yet you are still you.
Steady. Constant. A river.
Grant me peace like a river,
That I might be able to come to the bank
And dip my toes in the water with my friends.
Amen

act

I Am. Inside the *H* in your sketch space, write an "I Am" poem. This is simple. Write 10 statements beginning with the words *I am*. Fill the remaining sketch space with names of friends—maybe members of your creative community. Beside their names write statements of things they are gifted with. Then make a point that day to tell them what you wrote. If you have any remaining sketch space, journal about this experience and take time to pray about what it means to become the body of Christ with many important parts.

Change the energy settings on your computer so it is not expending large amounts of energy while you are doing other things.

sketch

pray

THIS MORNING I PRAY…

Holy Spirit,
Give me *shalom*.
Amen

THIS DAY I PRAY…

Holy Spirit,
I will rejoice and rejoice,
For you are always near.
I will transform my worries into
    humble requests,
And I will leave them to you.
I will not carry around the weight of things
    I can't understand.
I will allow these burdens to rest in
    your capable hands.
Amen

THIS NIGHT I PRAY…

Christ Jesus,
Guard my heart.
Guard my mind.
Amen

act

Inside the *I* in your sketch space, jot down some words or images that represent the anxieties in your life. Then choose a color that you feel best represents peace and use crayons, colored pencils, markers, whatever to fill the remaining space around the *I* with your anxious thoughts. Pray about what it would look like to live this out—surrounding your anxieties with God's infinite peace, which surpasses understanding.

Save packaging materials you receive in the mail and from others to use later to pack your own boxes and presents.

sketch

pray

THIS MORNING I PRAY…
Holy Spirit,
Give me *shalom*.
Amen

THIS DAY I PRAY…
Holy Spirit,
Draw us to the sound of your playing.
Being tuned in this way means growing up;
No longer being an infant in my faith
But instead removing the training wheels
And making movements in step with your music.
Prepare us.
Amen

THIS NIGHT I PRAY…
Father God,
I will follow where you lead.
Help me practice the art of submission
Every day.
Amen

act

Place two words inside the *N* in your sketch space. *LEAD US.* Gather with your creative community and come up with an act of love you can display in your community, allowing the Spirit to lead you as the body of Christ. Use your remaining sketch space to journal about this experience.

 **Inspire one of your friends to start a garden** by giving the gift of a potted vegetable plant.

sketch

pray

THIS MORNING I PRAY…

Holy Spirit,
Give me *shalom*.
Amen

THIS DAY I PRAY…

Holy Spirit,
I need only give an account for myself.
So what good is it for me to judge?
What need is there for me to build walls?
What good does it do to magnify our differences?
We all belong to the Lord.
So what am I to do?
Just love.
Help me to set all else aside
And just love.
Amen

THIS NIGHT I PRAY…

Father God,
"It is written:
'As surely as I live,' says the Lord,
'every knee will bow before me;
every tongue will confess to God.' So then, each
of us will give an account of himself to God.
Therefore let us stop passing judgment on
one another. Instead, make up your mind not
to put any stumbling block or obstacle in your
brother's way."
—Romans 14:11-13 (NIV)
Amen

act

Judge Not. Spend some time this week with someone of another faith or belief system than your own—maybe even sharing a meal with his or her family. Make sure the time is substantial enough to facilitate good conversation about what you believe and what they believe. Do this with two main intentions: to love that person as God does and to know that person better. Outside the G in your sketch space, jot down some thoughts you had about this person before your experience. Inside the G, jot down some thoughts you have now.

 Don't throw away your old cell phones. They can be recycled. Do some research on a place you can go and turn in your old phone. You may even make some money in the process.

sketch

Here is a trustworthy saying that deserves full acceptance: Christ Jesus came into the world to save sinners—of whom I am the worst. But for that very reason I was shown mercy so that in me, the worst of sinners, Christ Jesus might display his unlimited patience as an example for those who would believe on him and receive eternal life. Now to the King eternal, immortal, invisible, the only God, be honor and glory for ever and ever. Amen.

—1 TIMOTHY 1: 15-17 (NIV)

pray

THIS MORNING I PRAY…
Holy Spirit,
Give me *shalom.*
Amen

THIS DAY I PRAY…
Holy Spirit,
Fill me to the brim and then even more so,
That I might be evidence of the statement:
Grace changes everything.
Rest around us.
Amen

THIS NIGHT I PRAY…
Prayer from page 6

act

Grace. Flip back through the pages of the Satisfied section you are now coming to the end of. What do the pages spell out? Write this down in your sketch space. As you flip through, think about your experience in this episode. What have you learned? What questions do you still have? What does the statement *GRACE CHANGES EVERYTHING* mean to you now? Today, tell a friend a story about grace.

sketch

PLEASE GO TO PAGE 6 FOR MORNING PRAYER

sketch

mission

pray

act

THIS MORNING I PRAY...

Father,
Unite me with my brothers and sisters.
Make us one in thought and mind.
Clear our spirits of any judgmental behavior.
Help us to be one body moving forward,
All in response to one great love.
Amen

THIS DAY I PRAY...

Jesus, my Savior,
In response to the poor and the rich,
Make us one.
In response to the weak and the strong,
Make us one.
In response to friend and foe,
Make us one.
In good times and in bad times,
Make us one.
Make us one.
Amen

THIS NIGHT I PRAY...

Holy Spirit,
Capture my heart.
Amen

The Body Dismembered. Read Acts 2:1-12 and then 1 Corinthians 1:10 with a pen or pencil in hand. As you read, use your sketch space to jot down some things that bother you about the church you attend, your youth group, your creative community, or your entire community—maybe even the world. Think about God's original vision for the church and what keeps us from that unity.

Write a short note of petition on a piece of notebook paper to the body of people you thought of as you read, outlining the things that need to change to establish oneness. You may decide to join with others and share your note, or you may want to offer your petition to God on your own. A suggestion: *do both.*

In your mission to inspire others to be more environmentally conscious, have you forgotten about your church? Ask if you can meet with your pastor and discuss some ideas for making the church healthier for the environment.

sketch

pray

THIS MORNING I PRAY...
Father,
I pray that I might share your dreams.
I know that it is bold to say,
But I pray it with all my heart,
That you might penetrate my finite mind
With the infinitely huge dreams you have,
And that my community and my church
Would be used to spread your dreams
To places and in ways I can't imagine.
I pray to share your wildest dreams.
Amen

THIS DAY I PRAY...
Jesus, my Savior,
Take our fears and insecurities
And throw them into the garbage heap.
Replace them with a burning passion
To see your kingdom spread
Wherever there is need
And however you see fit.
Send us.
Amen

THIS NIGHT I PRAY...
Holy Spirit,
Capture my heart.
Amen

act

Join together with your creative community. Plan a time when you can go somewhere none of you have been before. It may be a service project in an area of town you haven't ever visited, volunteering with an organization you have heard of but never stepped foot in, or a meal at an establishment you haven't been to. As you do this, use your sketch space to document your groups members' behaviors as you guys adjust to a new place. What was uncomfortable or scary about it? What was exciting?

Sometime after or before this planned excursion, read the story of Saul's conversion (Acts 9:1-16). What does this say about God's dream for the church? What does it say about your comfort level as you join in God's dream?

 Draw a picture or write a little bit about the thing you are most proud of as you have become a better steward of creation. Maybe it is a huge and healthy tomato plant. Maybe it is the changes at your school.

sketch

175

pray

THIS MORNING I PRAY...

Father,
Strengthen us in the face of trouble.
Help our faith to be solid as rock,
That we might not stumble in front our mockers
But be flawless in our action
So that they might see our deeds
And glorify you.
Amen

THIS DAY I PRAY...

Jesus, my Savior,
Turn our eyes and ears to you,
So that no matter what the world may say
We are not changed,
And we are not changing.
Amen

THIS NIGHT I PRAY...

Holy Spirit,
Capture my heart.
Amen

act

Gather with your creative community. Discuss some of the projects you have done together during this experience. How do you feel you have embodied the church God dreams of? What have been the reactions of those around you? Have you had any negative backlash for your actions? If so, how has your group handled that? How did everyone feel about it? Use your sketch space to jot down some of the thoughts and feelings your group had.

Pray together.

If you don't already have one, ask if your creative community can be in charge of planting a garden at your church or churches. Get the whole congregation involved in this.

sketch

pray

THIS MORNING I PRAY…

Father,
Help us, as a body, to avoid false teaching.
Bind our hearts to the truth so tightly
That we are easily able to spot imposters.
Help us to be aware at all times in our faith
Because there are wolves all around us.
Amen

THIS DAY I PRAY…

Jesus, my Savior,
Give us the wisdom to name the beast.
Guide our actions after we have done so.
Make us, as a body of believers,
"shrewd as snakes and as innocent as doves."
Amen

THIS NIGHT I PRAY…

Holy Spirit,
Capture my heart.
Amen

act

Identify the Beast. Join together with your creative community. Discuss any false teachings you or your friends may have come in contact with. How did you determine them as such? What thoughts or emotions did this cause amongst your group? Read together Matthew 7:15-20. Use your sketch space to journal about this discussion. Pray together that you will be able to recognize the wolves among the sheep.

False teaching is also a problem in your quest for environmental holiness. This is why you should always back up your purchases and actions with good research and read labels for harmful ingredients, even on products that proclaim environmental friendliness.

sketch

177

pray

THIS MORNING I PRAY…

Father,
Create in us an open environment of prayer.
We believe that prayer can change things,
So we will bring our confessions to each other,
And we will pray for full redemption.
We will pray with confidence for full healing.
Find us to be righteous men and women
So that our prayers will be powerful and effective.
Amen

THIS DAY I PRAY…

Jesus, my Savior,
In our triumphs and our failures,
Make us one.
In our strengths and our weaknesses,
Make us one.
In our sadness and our laughter,
Make us one.
As a church and as a body,
Make us one.
Amen

THIS NIGHT I PRAY…

Holy Spirit,
Capture my heart.
Amen

act

Confess and Pray. Gather together with your creative community. Have a time of honest confession and prayer for one another. Use your sketch space to jot down some of your thoughts and emotions from this time.

 Set aside a time of prayer specifically for the planet. This may seem odd because we are used to praying for people and situations, but the earth and its creatures are in need of God's blessing as well. Confess your downfalls as a caretaker and ask for help in these areas.

sketch

pray

THIS MORNING I PRAY…
Father,
Thank you for the stories we share.
I pray that as we share them,
We might come to know you more.
Amen

THIS DAY I PRAY…
Jesus, my brother,
I will declare the stories of what you've done
To all who will listen.
I will always be singing your praises
Into the crowds.
You have done awesome things.
Amen

THIS NIGHT I PRAY…
Prayer from page 6

act

The Journey. You've come quite a long way. And it's not over by any means, but I bet God has been doing some crazy awesome things not only in your life but all around you has you have continued to pay attention. Grab your student guide and gather with your creative community to tell stories from the journey through A *World Unbroken*. Flip through the pages and allow your mind to pull up the memories of that project, that prayer, that face, and share openly.

In your sketch space, make up titles for the stories you wish to tell and list them. This way you won't forget when you gather with your friends. Use the remaining space to jot down some thoughts and emotions you had from this experience.

sketch

PLEASE GO TO PAGE 6 FOR MORNING PRAYER

sketch

THIS MORNING I PRAY…
Father,
Help me to be perfect as you are perfect.
This is my aim,
That I might give what I need to give
And place nothing between us,
So that you might be near to me.
Amen

THIS DAY I PRAY…
Jesus, my Savior,
Show me what you want me to leave behind
So that I can follow you unrestrained,
However hard it might be.
Awaken my spirit to the spaces between us,
And help me to bridge those gaps.
I honestly want to follow.
Amen

THIS NIGHT I PRAY…
Holy Spirit,
Overflow in me.
Amen

act

Picture-Perfect Christian. What does it look like to follow Jesus perfectly? Really, what does it look like? Use your sketch space to draw a picture of the perfect Jesus follower. What would he carry? What would she be surrounded by? What kind of shoes would he wear or not wear? Use your remaining sketch space to explain your drawing.

Read Matthew 19:16-21. What are Jesus' ideas about a perfect follower? What does this mean for you? *Hint: It might not mean exactly the same thing for you as it did for the rich young ruler.*

 What if your family never bought anything new? Sit down with your family and make a commitment together to keep a list of all items bought new. After a couple weeks, look at the list together and determine how you could take steps to pare it down by buying used items.

sketch

He has showed you, O man, what is good.
And what does the Lord require of you?
To act justly and to love mercy
and to walk humbly with your God.

—MICAH 6:8 (NIV)

pray

THIS MORNING I PRAY…
Father,
Each day you give me a choice.
To choose life over death;
To choose peace over despair;
To choose justice over oppression;
To choose mercy over condemnation;
You have shown me what is good.
Help me choose wisely.
Amen

THIS DAY I PRAY…
Jesus, my Savior,
You are a living example
Of a love that can change things.
Help me demonstrate that kind of love
To a world that has so many stories
Headed the wrong direction.
I pray that love might be the turning point.
Amen

THIS NIGHT I PRAY…
Holy Spirit,
Overflow in me.
Amen

act

Acts of Justice. In your sketch space, write the outline to a very short play. The play will have three acts. Act 1 will specify the conflict. This will be the unjust way of this world that has bothered your soul the most as you have journeyed through this experience. Maybe it's human trafficking, hunger and poverty, homelessness, water shortages, lack of education, environmental wounds, etc. Act 2 specifies the turning point. This is the way you can act out justice in big and small ways each day to have an effect on this injustice. Act 3 is the resolution. This is the dream for how things could be when the crisis is turned to glory. You may need a sheet of notebook paper.

 Make a conscious effort to use only recyclable or reusable items today.

pray

THIS MORNING I PRAY…

Father,
You have raised me to be decidedly different
From the culture around me.
I wasn't made to fit seamlessly.
Forgive my attempts to join the crowd.
Forgive me for becoming comfortable
    amongst the masses.
Form in me a deep sense of discomfort
    with the ways of the world.
Amen

THIS DAY I PRAY…

Jesus, my Savior,
Take my everyday life—
My eating,
My sleeping,
My hanging around,
My in-between times—
Pattern each moment
With the colors and lines of your dreams
For your follower.
Amen

THIS NIGHT I PRAY…

Holy Spirit,
Overflow in me.
Amen

act

Patterns. Join together with your creative community. Have someone read aloud Romans 12:1-2 (The Message or NIV—preferably both); then discuss it. What does it mean to conform to the patterns of this world? In what ways do you struggle with this?

After the discussion, take some time to draw a pattern in your sketch space. You may need colored pencils or crayons. Have the elements of your pattern represent the elements of your everyday life; then share your patterns with each other.

Notice two things: How many elements in your pattern are things associated with the culture in which you navigate? Was anyone's pattern the same?

Changing patterns in your life is hard, especially if you try to do it all at once. This month, commit to replacing one thing you buy at the grocery with an organic substitute. Try to do the same each month.

sketch

pray

THIS MORNING I PRAY...

Father,
Above all else,
Show me your visions of love.
Show me how to live it out.
If I can't do that, then none of this matters.
Though the evil around me is menacing,
Love is and will always be greater.
Help me overcome evil with love.
Amen

THIS DAY I PRAY...

Jesus, my Savior,
Protect me from the evil one,
For he surrounds me.
His grip on this world is almost suffocating—
Almost.
Displays of your love disarm him.
Show him to be what he is—
A liar and a coward
Who cowers in the weeds when the Lion shows his face.
I praise you because I am with the Lion.
Amen

THIS NIGHT I PRAY...

Holy Spirit,
Overflow in me.
Amen

act

Love Assignments. Join together with your creative community. Read together Romans 12:9-21. As you read, use your sketch space to make each verse into a list of to-do's. Then assign each number on the list to a member of the group, placing a name next to each display of love. The assignment: Act it out this week in some way and then report back to the group. Smaller groups may have to assign each person more than one.

In your personal prayer time, think about the evil you have become more aware of in this world as you have journeyed through the *World Unbroken* experience. Pray on this.

Take two fewer car trips a week than is your normal schedule. After this week, see if you can cut out even more.

mission 12

pray

THIS MORNING I PRAY...
Father,
Turn me away from my own self-pity.
Take me from my own self-doubt.
Remove me from my own self-anything!
Turn me toward constant praise,
Constant prayer,
And enduring joy because of who you are.
Amen

THIS DAY I PRAY...
Jesus, my Savior,
What good are these burdens?
They only weigh me down.
They stifle my shouts of praise
And cause my feet to drag.
I lay it down and pick up yours,
For your yoke is easy, and your burden is light.
Amen

THIS NIGHT I PRAY...
Holy Spirit,
Overflow in me.
Amen

act

You Are My Joy. Use your sketch space to write a song of joy. You may not be musical. You may think it is stupid. Doesn't matter. Do it anyway. Write lyrics and think up a tune and then sing it to yourself. But that's not it. Join with a couple friends and sing your songs to each other. It doesn't matter what mood you were in before. I guarantee you will be laughing (or at least smiling) by the end.

Use your remaining sketch space to jot down why these things seem impossible to you: enduring joy, constant praise, and constant prayer.

Washing your laundry with cold water is an easy way to save energy. There are even special detergents for cold-water washes.

sketch

pray

THIS MORNING I PRAY…

Father,
Help me demonstrate true perseverance
By not just making it through rough times
But turning those times into glory.
Amen

THIS DAY I PRAY…

Jesus, my Savior,

"Now when he saw the crowds,
he went up on a mountainside and sat down.
His disciples came to him,
and he began to teach them saying:
'Blessed are the poor in spirit,
for theirs is the kingdom of heaven.
Blessed are those who mourn, for they will be comforted.
Blessed are the meek, for they will inherit the earth.
Blessed are those who hunger and thirst for righteousness,
for they will be filled.
Blessed are the merciful, for they will be shown mercy.
Blessed are the pure in heart, for they will see God.
Blessed are the peacemakers,
for they will be called sons of God.
Blessed are those who are persecuted because of righteousness,
for theirs is the kingdom of heaven.
Blessed are you when people insult you, persecute you and falsely
say all kinds of evil against you because of me. Rejoice and be glad,
because great is your reward in heaven, for in the same way they
persecuted the prophets who were before you.'"
—Matthew 5:1-12

Amen

THIS NIGHT I PRAY…
Prayer from page 6

act

Research and Reflect. Take some time to research the lives of the disciples and the apostle Paul after the death, resurrection, and ascension of Christ. Use your sketch space to take some notes. What can you learn about Jesus' vision for Christians from the outcome of their lives? This may be confusing for you. Get together with friends and discuss it.

Think on this: *What role does perseverance play in your spiritual life?*

 **Are you aware of the big environmental issues affecting our world today and the organizations that are working to fix things?** A big part of being environmentally conscious is educating yourself about these things and finding out what you can do to help. Do some research and use your sketch space to list the names of a couple organizations that catch your attention and what you can do to partner with them.

sketch

PLEASE GO TO PAGE 6 FOR MORNING PRAYER

sketch

pray

THIS MORNING I PRAY…

Father,
Lead us in your mission.
Allow your love to become tangible in this world,
Through us.
And allow our response to the gospel to be genuine
And unrelenting love for our neighbors.
Amen

THIS DAY I PRAY…

Jesus, my Savior,
We live in response to your grace.
I pray that we might forget that there is any other way.
Allow the rhythm of our lives to be set to the beat
Of the continuation of your ministry.
Help us to be good stewards of your grace.
Amen

THIS NIGHT I PRAY…

Holy Spirit,
Move through us.
Amen

act

Change. Join together with your creative community and talk. Do you remember why you originally began this group? You may need to look back through your guidebook to remember. Discuss this for a bit. How has it gone?

At the top of your sketch space, write this word: *CHANGE.* Think about that word together. What does it mean? How does it happen? Can it happen?

Today will mark a change in the purpose of your creative community. From now on, your every meeting will be centered around one mission: living out the gospel in your household, community, and world. You have been doing this already, but today recommit yourselves to weekly meetings where, together, you are always coming up with new ways to act out God's love and carry out his mission. Use your sketch space to jot down some thoughts and emotions you had during this meeting.

 Use your remaining sketch space to list some things that have changed in the way you view the environment since you began this experience.

sketch

pray

THIS MORNING I PRAY…

Father,
Guide me to those who know you well.
I was not meant to do this alone.
Help me find mentors and leaders,
Elders who will bring a perspective I need to see.
May I grow in respect and adoration for them
As I listen to and learn from their stories.
Amen

THIS DAY I PRAY…

Jesus, my Savior,
Surround me with a great cloud of witnesses.
Help me recognize and ignore the posers and
    phonies
And be drawn to those who have genuinely sought
    after you,
So that I might listen and be led
And grow up in you.
Amen

THIS NIGHT I PRAY…

Holy Spirit,
Move through us.
Amen

act

Respect Your Elders. Use your sketch space to jot down some names of older believers whom you think might make good mentors for you. Then pray about it. After you have spent time in prayer, ask the person you decide upon if he or she might have time to meet with you weekly over coffee, sodas, sushi, whatever.

This will be a time for you to share the struggles you are going through in your faith, the questions you have, and the experiences you don't know what to do with. Mostly this will be a time for you to listen to your mentor and to pray.

Collecting cans at lunch in your cafeteria is an easy way to make sure they get recycled. Have fun with it, maybe making can costumes to wear when you walk around with your recycling bag.

pray

THIS MORNING I PRAY...

Father,
Father me.
Conduct the music of my life.
Find in me an obedient daughter/son
No matter how much I may dislike it.
Draw me away from frivolous, fleeting things
To the things that actually matter.
Amen

THIS DAY I PRAY...

Jesus, my Savior,
Take me away from the mindset of fitting you in.
Instead, be the center of all I do
So that all I do would align with your dreams
Of justice and mercy for all.
Draw me away from the frivolous, fleeting things
To the things that actually matter.
Amen

THIS NIGHT I PRAY...

Holy Spirit,
Move through us.
Amen

act

Time for What Matters. Remember your three-act play of justice? You may need to turn back in your book to find it. You probably had more than one action that you thought of to bring about the turning point. Divide your sketch space into two sections. In one section, place all the actions you thought of but never were able to do. And in the other, place the things that take up your time and keep you from doing those things.

Maybe it's sports teams, clubs, hobbies, TV shows, shopping, etc. Then pray about it and begin to decide what can be crossed out on the list of things that take up your time. Replace the crossed-out things with the turning-point actions.

Join with your creative community and volunteer to clean up garbage after school events, such as dances or sports games. This way your group can make sure that the large amount of garbage from these special occasions is properly separated and recycled.

sketch

pray

THIS MORNING I PRAY…

Father,
Give me the ability to see beyond myself.
Help me invest in those younger than me.
Help me pour my life into them
So that they can learn from my story
And understand you more.
Amen

THIS DAY I PRAY…

Jesus, my Savior,
I pray that I might be about making disciples
Because this is your way.
Give me the wisdom to guide
And the humility to share my mistakes.
Help me see my story as one worth sharing,
And I pray that you would bless those who receive it.
Amen

THIS NIGHT I PRAY…

Holy Spirit,
Move through us.
Amen

act

Making Disciples. Use your sketch space to write down three names. These names will represent three younger people you have decided to invest in. Pray about this, and then go inform them of what has been laid on your heart for them. You may do this as a single group or with each individually. The important thing is that you schedule a time each week to meet and talk about faith, life, struggles, experiences, whatever.

Use your remaining sketch space to document your first initial meeting with the three people you chose. What was their reaction? Then, under their names, write down a prayer you can flip back to and pray for them whenever you feel so led.

Get together with one or more of the people from your list of names and plant something together. This way you can take equal responsibility for nurturing the plant, tree, or flower as your relationship strengthens. Use your remaining sketch space to draw a picture of the thing you planted in full bloom.

sketch

pray

THIS MORNING I PRAY...

Father,
I pray for those who are far from me.
Open my eyes to global concerns
And bring them near to me.
Those countries that are hurting,
Your children who are struggling.
Help me to see them with your eyes
And feel how you feel
So that I am simply unable to ignore them.
Draw me to them.
Amen

THIS DAY I PRAY...

Jesus, my Savior,
I have been petitioned to spread your love
    to edges of the earth.
Show me how to do it.
Help me be courageous in seeking justice
    for those in need.
I pray that my fears in taking steps
    toward justice
Might be overwhelmed by the fear that
    justice wouldn't come.
Amen

THIS NIGHT I PRAY...

Holy Spirit,
Move through us.
Amen

act

Living Mission. Use your sketch space to draw a picture, write a paragraph, or list some words that define what mission means to you. By now, you have come to understand that living out God's mission isn't just about traveling to a far-off country for a couple weeks a year to paint some walls with your friends. Mission is a *lifestyle*. Use your remaining sketch space to write down some ways you have allowed God's mission to impact the way you live your everyday life.

Yet an important part of living mission is being aware of and learning more about global causes. What has God laid on your heart in this area? What are you doing about it?

Join together with your creative community and talk about starting a social-networking site that shares your journey toward environmental holiness and opens space for discussion on green topics. Include tips, photos, discussion questions, and opportunities for others to get involved.

sketch

pray

THIS MORNING I PRAY…

Father,

I pray that something new would be born in me
And that these days might mark a new promise.
From here on, I will see others as you see others.
I will dream as you dream and love as you love.
I will never go back to the way things were.
Use my imagination to change things.
Amen

THIS DAY I PRAY…

Jesus, my Savior,
I thank you
For all you have done,
For all you are doing,
For all you are going to do.
Amen

THIS NIGHT I PRAY…

Prayer from page 6

act

Leave. Write that word *big* in your sketch space. Then decorate it with words or images. What does it mean to you? Whether you know it, if you have stuck through this whole *World Unbroken* experience, you have been on a pilgrimage. A pilgrimage is a search that holds great spiritual or moral importance. It is a journey away from the norm that changes a person for good.

Now it is time to take an actual trip. Here are some suggestions:

Get together with some members of your creative community and go on a weekend road trip.

Take a one-day trip with a mentor or friend to a park or some other quiet place.

Commit to spending an hour a day outside, amongst creation, all by yourself.

Be creative. Whatever you do, make sure of these things: that you are leaving the normal rhythm of your life, that you are reflecting on your pilgrimage, and that you are opening up a space for God to show himself to you.

 An easy way that you can cut down on plastic and Styrofoam use while you're traveling is to buy a travel mug that you can refill with beverages at restaurants and gas stations.

sketch

PLEASE GO TO PAGE 6 FOR MORNING PRAYER

sketch

pray

THIS MORNING I PRAY…

Father,
Allow my house to be a place of stewardship.
I pray that it would begin here, in my life,
And that people would see my actions and
    do likewise.
Instill in my family a rhythm of environmental care.
Amen

THIS DAY I PRAY…

Jesus, my Savior,
Help me be careful and intentional
In all that I do.
In my relationships with others and the earth,
May I be relentless in my obedience
So that my actions bring glory to your name
In all the earth.
Amen

THIS NIGHT I PRAY…

Holy Spirit,
Be seen in us.
Amen

act.

Cleaning House. Use your sketch space to list five additional environmental changes you can still make in your household. Whether it's big or small, use the remaining space to jot down some ideas on how to implement these changes and how your family can stay accountable to each other in making these changes consistent habits.

List five ways you can use your household to reach out to those in need and the community. Have the same discussion about how you can make these a consistent habit.

 Look around you right now. What lights are on that could be turned off? If any, get up and turn them off.

sketch

pray

THIS MORNING I PRAY...

Father,
I pray that the work of my hands would be good,
That I would live as though I am preparing a place
For my neighbors—my brothers and sisters.
Instill in my friends and me a discipline of
    restorative action,
That we would always see things as they could be,
Always dreaming.
Amen

THIS DAY I PRAY...

Jesus, my Savior,
You dug your hands into the soil
So that we might be healed.
You healed with your hands,
Not from a distance.
Help us to do the same
For the wounds of creation that we pass each day.
Help us never to be okay with a clean-handed faith.
Amen

THIS NIGHT I PRAY...

Holy Spirit,
Be seen in us.
Amen

act

Seek and Restore. Gather together with your creative community. Use your sketch space as you brainstorm together about some place in your community that is in need of restoration. Maybe it is a building, a garden, a park, or a house. Decide on one place and come up with a cool way that your group can transform it into a positive place in your community instead of an eyesore. Use your remaining sketch space to lay out your plans with pictures or words.

Take a picture of the place your group chose before its restoration. Blow up the picture and print it off. Use crayons or markers to draw over the top of the picture a portrayal of what your dream for the place would be. Share your pictures with the group and discuss them.

Walk, run, or bike somewhere today instead of driving.

sketch

pray

THIS MORNING I PRAY…

Father,
With the provisions you have given me,
More than I deserve,
I pray that I might go about the mission
Of seeing those who are hungry fed
And those who are thirsty satisfied.
Amen

THIS DAY I PRAY…

Jesus, my Savior,
Because I love you,
I will feed your lambs.
Because I love you,
I will take care of your sheep.
Because I love you,
I will feed your sheep.
Because you loved me first,
I will honor you by serving others.
Amen

THIS NIGHT I PRAY…

Holy Spirit,
Be seen in us.
Amen

act

Preparations. Make a meal for someone. Use your sketch space to write down the recipe you use. Maybe it is just a PB&J sandwich. As you do this, pray. How do you think preparing a meal relates to God's mission? Use your sketch space to write down some thoughts or emotions you had from this experience.

 Begin packing your lunch every day. Do some research on how you can do this using all reusable items.

sketch

THIS MORNING I PRAY…
Father,
Make me like an empty vessel today.
Help me resolve the conflicts
And run from the temptations
That distract me from your mission.
Instill in me the kind of peace
That makes me a better servant.
Amen

THIS DAY I PRAY…
Jesus, my Savior,
Help me grow up in you.
Instill in me the spirit of a smart builder
So I might live within your words
And build a home there.
Amen

THIS NIGHT I PRAY…
Holy Spirit,
Be seen in us.
Amen

act

Resolution. When there are lingering things in your life—whether it is conflict with a person or sins you have been unable to confess to a friend—your spirit gets bogged down and heavy. These things make it easy to feel far from God and easy to worry about your own life rather than the mission of God. Use this day to alleviate your spirit of unneeded weight. Say you're sorry, call the person you've been avoiding, make things right so you are prepared to go on from here, free from the constraints of a troubled spirit.

Use your sketch space to write a short journal entry about this experience. Title it "_____ Resolution." Before you write, think on these things: *Why are we built this way? Why do we feel better when conflict is resolved and the air is clear?*

Spend some time at your adopted spot in nature today. Breathe in and out. Use your sketch space to draw a picture of all that you see, or maybe write some words of praise to God because of his amazing creation all around you.

sketch

pray

THIS MORNING I PRAY…

Father,
How deep is your love
That you might give all you have for us.
In response, I submit myself to you
And pray that all the power and glory would be
    yours.
Amen

THIS DAY I PRAY…

Jesus, my Savior,
How deep is your love,
That you might endure the humiliation of the cross.
In response, I submit myself to you.
Replace my lust for power
With a daily commitment to laying down my life.
Instill in me a discipline of disempowerment.
And may all the power and glory be yours.
Amen

THIS NIGHT I PRAY…

Holy Spirit,
Be seen in us.
Amen

act

Daily Disempowerment. Write the word *power* at the top of your sketch space then divide it into two sections. Think of a few people whom you feel display power. Then in one column, place some words or images that define them. On the other side, place some words or images that define the kind of power Jesus exhibited. What is the difference? What does this say about the kind of power we are supposed to show?

 Join together with your creative community and adopt a stretch of highway or a park where your group can commit to trash pickup. Have everyone carry two bags—one for recyclable items.

sketch

His divine power has given us everything we need for life and godliness through our knowledge of him who called us by his own glory and goodness. Through these he has given us his very great and precious promises, so that through them you may participate in the divine nature and escape the corruption in the world caused by evil desires.

For this very reason, make every effort to add to your faith goodness; and to goodness, knowledge; and to knowledge, self-control; and to self-control, perseverance; and to perseverance, godliness; and to godliness, brotherly kindness; and to brotherly kindness, love. For if you possess these qualities in increasing measure, they will keep you from being ineffective and unproductive in your knowledge of our Lord Jesus Christ. But if anyone does not have them, he is nearsighted and blind, and has forgotten that he has been cleansed from his past sins.

Therefore, my brothers, be all the more eager to make your calling and election sure. For if you do these things, you will never fall, and you will receive a rich welcome into the eternal kingdom of our Lord and Savior Jesus Christ.

—2 PETER 1:3-11 (NIV)

pray

THIS MORNING I PRAY...

Father,
Speak to me with divine power.
Give me the ability to listen
To what you would have me do.
Give me the desire to see it done.
Instill in me a heart of mission.
Amen

THIS DAY I PRAY...

Jesus, my Savior,
Welcome me in.
Amen

THIS NIGHT I PRAY...

Prayer from page 6

act

Increasing Measure. Gather together with a few friends. Read 2 Peter 1: 3-11 and discuss the attributes that should be added to faith. Which do you struggle most with? Share this with the group. Then, one at a time, share a calling you feel God has laid on your heart. It might not be a life calling. It might be a calling for the next hour of your day. It doesn't matter. Share with each other what you have heard from God through this experience. Then discuss this question: How important is listening to your faith?

Use your sketch space to take notes from this discussion.

 **What environmental issues have you felt most called to over the course of this experience?** Draw in your remaining sketch space some picture of how this could affect the rest of your life as you move on from here.

sketch

PLEASE GO TO PAGE 6 FOR MORNING PRAYER

sketch

sketch

In the next section, you are encouraged to take this experience into your own hands. Allow Scripture to guide you and the Holy Spirit to lead you.

Write your own prayers, brainstorm your own actions, and sketch to your heart's content.

In short, the training wheels are off. You want *A World Unbroken*. Go, and make it so.

restored

pray

act

Read John 1:1-5 (THE MESSAGE).

Extreme Listening. Things will be different from now on. It is as if you are listening with new ears. Thinking and imagining with a renewed mind. Speaking and acting with a spirit that is not your own.

So I dare you now to listen extremely. Spend this week without speaking. Commit yourself to silence and listening. Inform your teachers, parents, friends—whoever needs to know—of your plan and purpose. Daily scripture will guide you through your entire *World Unbroken* experience.

Your daily prayer, action, and sketch spaces will be empty but not for long. You will fill them with the outpourings of your spirit as you observe and listen to God's activity all around you.

This won't be easy, and if you can only bear a single day or an hour a day in silence, that is okay, but I dare you to try the whole week to be speechless before God. See what happens.

sketch

"Listen, I tell you a mystery:
We will not all sleep, but we
will all be changed."

—1 CORINTHIANS 15:51 (NIV)

pray

act

Read Hosea 8.

sketch

pray

act

Read Leviticus 26:3-13 (THE MESSAGE) and Isaiah 43:1-3 (NIV).

sketch

pray

act

Read Isaiah 7:13 (THE MESSAGE), Here's a story that you may know... Daniel 3:4-29 (THE MESSAGE) and Matthew 1:1-25 (THE MESSAGE).

sketch

pray

act.

Read Matthew 15:29-38 (The Message), Luke 22:14-20 (THE MESSAGE) and
1 Timothy 1:15-17 (NIV).

sketch

pray

act

Read Mark 12:41-44 (THE MESSAGE) and Matthew 5-7 (The Message).

sketch

pray

THIS MORNING I PRAY...

PRAYER FROM PAGE 6

Read Isaiah 65:17-25 (THE MESSAGE).

sketch

act

Going Forth. Maybe you have already come to understand that this is just the beginning. This last week of your *World Unbroken* experience shouldn't be the last week. When the pages end, the rhythm will remain. Embrace it.

Use your prayer space this week to write out your petitions and praise to God. The action space will be filled with habits to remember as you go forth. The sketch space will spell out the word *RESTORE*. Think about that word. Let it bounce around in your mind. What did it mean to you before? What does it mean now?

Remember all that you've learned and the one who has been and will be with you. You will never be alone. Now listen and lead on.

Create a space for daily prayer and meditation. Determine a way to include others in your personal prayer life. This may be through a small group, accountability partner, or meetings with a mentor.

sketch

pray

act

Confess. Practice public confession daily. No, I don't mean using a megaphone. Confess to friends about the things you are struggling with. Go first. Your vulnerability, believe it or not, will make you a more valuable leader for the kingdom.

sketch

pray

act

Promise. Document and share with others a promise that God has laid on your heart during this process: what does it require of you? What is God saying will happen if you are faithful? This isn't testing God. If you are truly listening, you will know his promise is genuine.

sketch

pray

act.

Time. Ask God how you can be more generous with your time as you act upon the impressions on your heart. This may mean doing some things you have never had interest in and giving up things that meant a lot at one point but now seem like frivolous and selfish pursuits. Do the same with your resources. This doesn't mean money only; do you have gifts and abilities to offer God that you have been holding back?

sketch

act

Breaking Bread. Begin a weekly meal in your community. This could mean a meal with friends that is absolutely mandatory, a breakfast for the homeless that you bring to them, an after-school dinner club, etc. Be creative. Make sure that the taking of holy communion is a part of this meal every time, regardless of setting or attendees.

sketch

pray

act

Move. Start a movement. There is no doubt that during this process, God has sparked in you a deep desire for change in some aspect of this world. Latch onto that and be creative in what you do next. A movement is when people of like ideas come together to advance something forward.

sketch

pray

THIS MORNING I PRAY...

PRAYER FROM PAGE 6

act

sketch

E

sketch

sketch

sketch

sketch

sketch